by the Society of
Wine Educators

SOCIETY
of WINE
EDUCATORS

CERTIFIED
SPECIALIST
OF SPIRITS

**WORKBOOK
2020**
To Accompany the
2020 CSS Study Guide

The Society of Wine Educators (SWE) is a membership-based nonprofit organization focused on providing wine and spirits education along with the conferral of several certifications. The Society is internationally recognized, and its programs are highly regarded for both their quality and relevance to the industry.

The mission of the SWE is to set the standard for quality and responsible wine and spirits education and professional certification.

With its diverse programs, SWE is unique among educational programs in the wine and spirits field. Each year, the Society presents an annual conference with over 50 educational sessions and significant opportunities for professional interaction. Education and networking are further enhanced through symposiums, the Society's newsletter, and robust social media efforts.

SWE offers four professional credentials for those seeking to certify their wine and spirits knowledge, including the Certified Specialist of Wine (CSW), the Certified Specialist of Spirits (CSS), the Certified Wine Educator (CWE), and the Certified Spirits Educator (CSE). In addition, the Hospitality/Beverage Specialist Certificate is available, offered both as a self-study guide and an online class.

SWE members include the following types of individuals:

- Educators offering classes and tastings
- Instructors in public and private colleges, universities, and hospitality schools
- Importers, distributors, and producers
- Retailers, restaurateurs, and hoteliers
- Industry consultants
- Sommeliers, wine stewards, bartenders, and mixologists
- Culinary and hospitality school students
- Wine and spirits industry media professionals
- Wine and spirits enthusiasts

For more information about the Society's educational and membership programs, please contact us.

Society of Wine Educators
Telephone: (202) 408-8777
Website: www.societyofwineeducators.org

This publication is intended to provide accurate information with regard to the subject matter covered; however, the world of alcoholic beverages is a volatile one, and facts, figures, laws, consumption levels, and other information regarding these products are all liable to change over time. Please contact the Society of Wine Educators if you have any questions or comments about the contents of this guide.

The answer key for this workbook is available online at SWE's blog site at http://winewitandwisdomswe.com/study-guide-updates/csw-workbook-answer-key/.

Printed in the United States of America

INTRODUCTION TO THE CERTIFIED SPECIALIST OF SPIRITS WORKBOOK

The Certified Specialist of Spirits (CSS) certification represents the Society of Wine Educators' recognition that the holder has attained an in-depth knowledge about distillation and the major spirits categories, as well as the art of service as it applies to distilled spirits. The CSS Study Guide, published by the Society of Wine Educators, is the approved study tool for the CSS and covers the depth of information needed to successfully pass the CSS Certification Exam.

This workbook is intended to accompany the 2020 version of the CSS Study Guide. Used properly, this workbook should be an invaluable tool for all CSS candidates. The chapters in this workbook follow the chapters in the CSS Study Guide. These exercises are intended both to assess your comprehension and to increase your memory retention of the subject matter. These exercises are organized according to the major topic headings within the Study Guide itself.

We recommend that you first read and study a chapter in the Study Guide, and then complete the exercises in the workbook. After you read the chapter, try to answer the questions without consulting the Study Guide, and then check your answers by using the online answer key. Each chapter's exercises include a short "checkpoint" quiz intended to test your knowledge after you have completed your study of the chapter.

Keep in mind that while the exercises in this workbook cover much of the information found in our Study Guide, any information found in the Study Guide (chapters 1–12) is considered fair game to be used as the basis for questions found on the Certified Specialist of Spirits Exam.

ANSWER KEY

The answer key for this workbook is available online at SWE's blog site at http://winewitandwisdomswe.com/study-guide-updates/csw-workbook-answer-key/.

A NOTE ON MAPS AND DIAGRAMS

The maps and many of the diagrams in the CSS Study Guide are available electronically on the SWE Blog, *Wine, Wit, and Wisdom*. Candidates are encouraged to access these materials and to download full-page copies of the maps and diagrams for use in study. These materials are considered an integral part of the Study Guide, and candidates should expect that information from them will be included in the CSS Exam.

RESOURCES FOR CSS CANDIDATES

The Society of Wine Educators offers many resources for CSS students and exam candidates, including the following:

Webinars: Monthly SWEbinars are available at no charge and to the public, covering CSS- and CSW-related topics. For more information, including the schedule, see the SWEbinar webpage at SWE's blog, http://winewitandwisdomswe.com/.

Online Prep Classes: Several times a year, SWE offers guided, ten-week online prep classes covering the CSS Study Guide. These classes are offered free of charge for professional members of SWE who hold a current CSS Exam attendance credit. For more information, contact Jane Nickles at jnickles@societyofwineeducators.org.

Study Guide Updates: To assist all members of the adult beverage industry so that they may keep up with the ever-changing world of wine and spirits, SWE maintains Study Guide Updates pages for both the CSS and CSW Study Guides. Any changes that occur in the regulatory landscape, or elsewhere, that affect the information in the Study Guides will be updated on these pages. To access our Study Guide Updates page, see http://winewitandwisdomswe.com/study-guide-updates/.

CSS Exams: The CSS Exam consists of 100 multiple-choice questions, with all question content drawn exclusively from the CSS Study Guide. Candidates are provided with one (1) hour in which to complete the exam. Exams based on the 2020 version of the CSS Study Guide will be available at Pearson Vue Testing Centers through December 30, 2022. To find a Pearson VUE Center near you, use the search function on SWE's landing page at the Pearson VUE website: http://www.pearsonvue.com/societyofwineeducators/.

The Certified Spirits Educator Certification: SWE has recently launched a higher-level spirits certification, the Certified Spirits Educator (CSE). The CSE Exam is a unique certification that tests a candidate's knowledge of spirits, as well as his or her tasting acumen and teaching ability. This intense undertaking consists of a theory exam, two tasting exams, and a presentation skills demonstration, along with requiring candidates to provide evidence of Responsible Beverage Alcohol Service certification. All candidates pursuing the CSE certification must already possess the Certified Specialist of Spirits (CSS) certification. Candidates who successfully pass all components of the CSE Exam are entitled to use the CSE post-nominal as part of their professional signature. They will also receive a certificate (suitable for framing) and a CSE lapel pin. More information on the CSE is available on the SWE website.

A FINAL NOTE

We hope that this workbook is useful to you in your studies, and we wish you the best of luck as your prepare to sit for the certification exam. Hopefully, we will soon be able to welcome you into the ranks of Certified Specialists of Spirits!

CERTIFIED SPECIALIST OF SPIRITS

TABLE OF CONTENTS

SOCIETY
of WINE
EDUCATORS

SPIRIT PRODUCTION

LEARNING OBJECTIVES

After studying this chapter, the candidate should be able to do the following:
- Describe the processes of fermentation and distillation as they apply to the production of alcoholic beverages.
- Discuss the various types of stills and the impact that their use can have on the various styles of distilled beverages.

- Identify and describe the processes of spirit maturation, including aging in oak and other post-distillation procedures.
- Identify and describe the categorization of distilled spirits and other alcoholic beverages.

EXCERCISE 1: THE PRODUCTION OF DISTILLED SPIRITS: FILL IN THE BLANK/SHORT ANSWER

Fill in the blanks or provide a short answer for the following statements or questions.

1. What is the main type of alcohol present in alcoholic beverages? _____

2. In terms of alcohol, what is mean by the term *potable*?

   _____

3. Of the base ingredients used to produce alcoholic beverages, which ones contain readily available sugars?

   _____

4. Of the base ingredients used to produce alcoholic beverages, which ones require saccharification?

   _____

5. What is the boiling point of pure water? _____

6. What is the boiling point of pure ethyl alcohol? _____

7. In terms of alcohol and water, what does the term *miscible* mean?

   _____

8. What is the highest level of alcohol by volume achievable in commercial distillation?

   _____

EXERCISE 2: THE PRODUCTION OF DISTILLED SPIRITS: MATCHING

Match each of the following terms with its appropriate definition. Each term may be used more than once.

Proof	Wash	Heart
Dehydration	Vaporization	Cut points
Lees	Heads	
Congeners	Tails	

1. _____ A fermented liquid that is intended to be distilled into a spirit

2. _____ Procedure needed to achieve 100% alcohol by volume

3. _____ Acids, aldehydes, and other compounds created during fermentation that lend aromas and flavors to distilled products

4. _____ The transformation of a liquid into a gas

5. _____ Another name for the feints of a distillate

6. _____ Portion of a distillate that contains the foreshots

7. _____ A term used to describe the alcoholic strength of beverages

8. _____ The portion of the distillate that contains the potable spirit

9. _____ The dead yeast cells left over after fermentation is complete

10. _____ The portion of the distillate that contains high boilers

11. _____ The part of the distillate that contains low boilers

12. _____ Term used for the separation points between parts of the distillate

EXERCISE 3: THE POT STILL DIAGRAM

Using the diagram and the terms listed below; identify the parts of the pot still.

Exercise: Pot Still Diagram

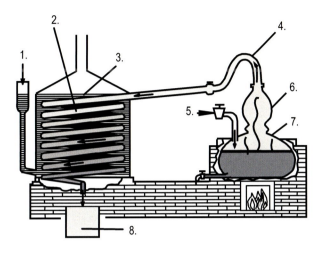

Figure 1.1: Pot still diagram exercise

Swan's neck   Collecting safe
Wash inlet   Water source
Copper pot   Worm condenser
Cooling water   Still head

1. _____

2. _____

3. _____

4. _____

5. _____

6. _____

7. _____

8. _____

Match each of the following terms with its appropriate definition. Each term will be used only once.

Multiple column still   Low wines   Rectifier   Robert Stein
Patent still   Reflux   Downcomer   Aeneas Coffey
Hybrid still   Analyzer   Brouillis
Pot still   Hydroselector column   Lyne Arm

1. _____   The type of still that works in the batch process

2. _____   Term used for the first batch of distillate in brandy production

3. _____   Term used for the first batch of distillate in whiskey production

4. _____   A technique used to control the parts of the liquid that are passed onto the condenser and those that are returned to the still

5. _____   Another term for a Coffey still

6. _____   Portion of a column still that includes the stripping section and the rectifying section

7. _____   Inventor of the 1826 version of the of the column still

8. _____   Another term for the purifier column

9. _____   Column of a still where the final distillation takes place

10. _____   Another term for a pot-and-column still

11. _____   Pipe that connects the plates inside a column still

12. _____   Inventor who re-engineered and "perfected" the column still

13. _____   Type of still able to produce spirits with the highest abv

14. _____   Portion of a pot still that carries the heated vapors from the neck of the still to the condenser

EXERCISE 5: THE SINGLE-COLUMN STILL: DIAGRAM EXERCISE

Using the diagram and the terms listed below, identify the parts of the single-column still.

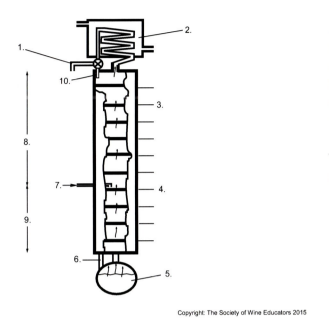

Copyright: The Society of Wine Educators 2015

Figure 1.2: Single-column still diagram exercise

Analyzer—stripping section
Analyzer—rectifying section
Liquid return
Condenser
Reflux tube
Boiler
Wash feed
10% abv product takeoff
50% abv product takeoff
High-alcohol product takeoff

1. _____

2. _____

3. _____

4. _____

5. _____

6. _____

7. _____

8. _____

9. _____

10. _____

EXERCISE 6: THE HYBRID STILL: DIAGRAM EXERCISE

Using the diagram and the terms listed below, identify the parts of the single-column still.

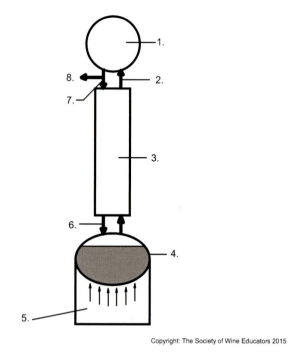

Copyright: The Society of Wine Educators 2015

Figure 1.3: Hybrid still diagram exercise

Product takeoff
Liquid return
Pot still
Alcohol vapor and water vapor
Heat source
Reflux
Condenser
Column still

1. _____

2. _____

3. _____

4. _____

5. _____

6. _____

7. _____

8. _____

EXERCISE 7: THE MATURATION OF DISTILLED SPIRITS: FILL IN THE BLANK/SHORT ANSWER

Fill in the blanks or provide a short answer for the following statements or questions.

1. What term is used for all newly distilled spirits? _____

2. What color are all newly distilled spirits? _____

3. What are some typical post-distillation treatments used in the production of spirits?

   _____

4. Identify the oak heartwood components described below:

   a. Helps "cement" the fiber cells in the wood together: _____

   b. Responsible for the "red layer" in charred barrels: _____

   c. Provides structural integrity and chemical resistance to the wood: _____

   d. Contains many sugars that are soluble in alcohol: _____

   e. Makes up 40% of the mass of the wood: _____

   f. Source of methoxyphenols: _____

5. The methoxyphenol group includes syringol and other compounds that smell and taste like

   _____

6. Identify the processes of oak aging described below:

   a. Occurs due to the presence of charcoal: _____

   b. Occurs due to the degrading of the tannins of the wood: _____

   c. Occurs due to the semiporous character of the wood: _____

   d. Adds aromas of chocolate, butterscotch, and caramel to the spirit:

   _____

   e. Results in the "angel's share": _____

EXERCISE 8: SPIRIT CATEGORIES: MATCHING

Match each of the following terms with its appropriate definition. Each term will be used only once.

Liqueurs   Rum   Tequila   Mirabelle   Pomace brandy
Whiskey   Cachaça   Mezcal   Akvavit   Amari
Brandy   Gin   Vodka   Vermouth

1. _____   A type of aromatized wine

2. _____   A spirit flavored with juniper berry

3. _____   A type of plum brandy

4. _____   General term used for spirits made with grain

5. _____   A spirit produced with the blue agave plant

6. _____   General term used for spirits made with sugar and sugar products

7. _____   Term used for a broad category of bittered spirits

8. _____   Typically a clear, water-white spirit with a neutral flavor profile

9. _____   A spirit flavored with caraway

10. _____   General term used for spirits made with fruit

11. _____   Sweetened, flavored spirits

12. _____   A spirit distilled from a range of agave varieties

13. _____   A type of rum

14. _____   A spirit made from the leftovers of winemaking

1. What is the typical alcohol content of a beverage fermented from grapes or other fruit?
    a. 2–6%
    b. 5–10%
    c. 8–14%
    d. 14–20%

2. What is the typical alcohol content of a beverage fermented from starchy grains?
    a. 2–6%
    b. 5–10%
    c. 8–14%
    d. 14–20%

3. What role do congeners play in the production of distilled spirits?
    a. They provide distinct aromas and flavors.
    b. They provide nutrients for the yeast during fermentation.
    c. They lower the boiling point of ethanol.
    d. They must be eliminated lest they cause the spirit to turn cloudy.

4. What is the boiling point of pure ethyl alcohol?
    a. 98°F/37°C
    b. 155°/68°C
    c. 173°F/78°C
    d. 212°F/100°C

5. What is the highest level of alcohol by volume that can be obtained via commercial distillation?
    a. 88.5%
    b. 92.8%
    c. 96.5%
    d. 99.9%

6. Which term is used to describe the last portion of the distillate run?
    a. Foreshots
    b. Low boilers
    c. Reflux
    d. High boilers

7. What is another name for a column still?
    a. Patent still
    b. Pot still
    c. Hybrid still
    d. Reboiler

8. Which of the following is part of the analyzer of a column still?
    a. The reflux tube
    b. The downcomer pipe
    c. The worm condenser
    d. The rectifying section

9. Of the following types of stills, which can produce the highest-proof distillate?
    a. Patent still
    b. Coffey still
    c. Multiple column still
    d. Single-column still

10. What color is a new-make spirit?
    a. Cloudy white
    b. Water-white
    c. It varies according to base materials used
    d. It varies according to the type of still used

11. The "red layer" of an oak barrel is composed mainly of what substance?
    a. Lignin
    b. Hemicellulose
    c. Cellulose
    d. Tannin

12. What is the average annual volume loss while a spirit ages in an oak barrel?
    a. 0.5%
    b. 3%
    c. 6%
    d. 10%

13. Which of the following processes of oak aging is most responsible for the formation of aldehydes?
    a. Oxidation
    b. Concentration
    c. Filtration
    d. Evaporation

14. Which of the following processes of oak aging results from the lowered volume of total spirit?
    a. Extraction
    b. Filtration
    c. Polymerization
    d. Concentration

15. What type of still works in a batch process?
    a. Spirit still
    b. Pot still
    c. Continuous still
    d. Patent still

LEARNING OBJECTIVES

After studying this chapter, the candidate should be able to do the following:

- Describe the process of the sensory evaluation of spirits as used by beverage professionals.
- Discuss the ideal setup of a distilled beverage tasting, including proper logistics, glassware, and the choice of beverage(s).

- Identify visual clues regarding the type and quality of distilled spirits.
- Recognize and describe the aromas, flavors, and tactile sensations exhibited by distilled spirits.
- Describe how complexity, finish, and quality are revealed during the spirits evaluation process.

EXERCISE 1: THE SENSORY EVALUATION OF SPIRITS: TRUE OR FALSE

Mark each of the following statements as true or false.

1. _____ The age of a spirit can always be determined by its color.

2. _____ While there are many styles of specialty glassware available, a typical white wine tasting glass is appropriate for most professional spirit-tasting sessions.

3. _____ In most cases, spirits should be tasted in order of alcohol by volume, from lowest to highest.

4. _____ In most cases, spirits should be tasted in order of age, from oldest to youngest.

5. _____ Spirits that are normally served cold, such as vodka or gin, must be served cold for the purposes of sensory evaluation.

6. _____ White spirits that are usually clear or watery in color may sometimes show a slight platinum hue.

7. _____ Diluting a spirit with a small amount of water often allows its aromas to blossom.

8. _____ The term *mouthfeel* is often used to denote the texture and weight of a spirit.

9. _____ In terms of taste impressions, bitterness tends to fade very quickly while sweetness lasts the longest of all.

Match each of the following terms with its appropriate definition. Each term will be used only once.

Meniscus	Louching	Alcohol	Sweetness
Complexity	Viscosity	Bitterness	Finish
Turbidity	Rancio	Acidity	Length

1. _____ The amount of time (short, medium, or long) that sensations remain on the palate

2. _____ Taste component generally sensed across the back of the palate

3. _____ 50% of the population perceives ethyl alcohol as having this taste component

4. _____ Visual effect that occurs when some spirits are mixed with water

5. _____ Term used to describe the oxidized character of certain spirits

6. _____ The edge of a spirit (or other liquid) in the glass

7. _____ Term used to describe a spirit with a good range of different aromas and flavors

8. _____ Taste component that causes a salivary reaction on the palate

9. _____ Component that tends to "propel" aromas forward out of the glass

10. _____ The collection of sensations that a spirit leaves on the palate

11. _____ Term used to describe the perception of whether a spirit feels "thick" or "thin"

12. _____ A cloudy or hazy appearance

EXERCISE 3: THE SENSORY EVALUATION OF SPIRITS: FILL IN THE BLANK/SHORT ANSWER

Fill in the blanks or provide a short answer for the following statements or questions.

1. Ideally, spirits should be evaluated in _____ of similar products, and with no more than _____ to _____ samples at a time.

2. The _____ that run down the sides of a glass after swirling may be indicative of the spirit's levels of sugar or _____.

3. If you can detect and describe the aromas of a spirit at a distance of six inches from the nose, the aromas can be classified as _____.

4. If a spirit's aromas can first be detected at a distance of three inches from the nose, they can be classified as _____, and if detecting the aromas requires that your nose be at the rim of the glass, they can be described as _____.

5. When evaluating spirits, most experts recommend that, instead of agitating a glass by "swirling" it, you give the glass a gentle _____.

6. By reducing the _____ strength of the spirit, dilution may allow some of the background flavors to come forward.

7. Taking a quick sip of a spirit and inhaling through the mouth before performing a sensory evaluation of a spirit may help to both prepare and _____ the palate.

8. In-mouth impressions may be described in terms of _____, such as silky or soft; _____, such as light, medium, or heavy; and _____, such as thick or thin.

9. The perception of _____ can often be derived from vanilla- and coconut-flavored compounds in a spirit.

10. Well-made spirits that evolve in the glass and reveal an array of sensations may be described as _____.

11. A spirit with a heavy perception of alcohol may be described as _____ or _____.

1. In the context of spirits, what is the meniscus?
   a. The middle, or eye, of the spirit as it is observed in the glass
   b. A unique haze that may be seen in a spirit that has been treated with caramel coloring
   c. A silver tint that may be observed in agave-based spirits
   d. The rim or edge of a spirit in the glass

2. Which of the following spirits is most likely to demonstrate the louche effect?
   a. Compound gin
   b. Absinthe
   c. Pot still whiskey
   d. Vodka

3. If you can detect and describe the aromas of a spirit at a distance of six inches from your nose, what term would you use to describe the aromatics?
   a. Intense
   b. Medium intense
   c. Light
   d. Extremely light

4. Which of the following is the best advice to follow when analyzing the aromas of a flight of spirits?
   a. If you have more than four spirits in a flight, analyze them in quick order without taking a break in between samples.
   b. Always use chilled spirits, and always serve the spirits over ice.
   c. Keep your mouth open in order to avoid a rush of alcohol into your nose and eyes.
   d. Give the glass a good "shake" and an agitated "swirl" in order to release the aromas evenly.

5. Which of the following flavors are likely to be imparted to spirits that are aged in charred oak barrels?
   a. Wheat and bran
   b. Vanilla and coconut
   c. Orange peel and dried fruit
   d. Dried flowers and tropical fruit

6. The level of _____ in a particular spirit can be determined by noting the salivary reaction of your palate.
   a. Bitterness
   b. Sweetness
   c. Alcohol
   d. Acidity

7. Which of the following glasses would be considered ideal for the sensory evaluation of a flight of aged cognac?
   a. Large brandy snifters of 12- to 14-ounce capacity
   b. Shot glasses of 1- to 2-ounce capacity
   c. Tulip-shaped glasses of 6- to 8-ounce capacity
   d. Rocks glasses of 10- to 12-ounce capacity

8. Which of the following would be the ideal flight for the sensory evaluation of spirits?
   a. A selection of six Irish whiskeys arranged in order of age, from youngest to oldest
   b. A selection of three vodkas served chilled and three gins served at room temperature
   c. A selection of bittered spirits arranged in order of alcohol by volume, from highest to lowest
   d. A selection of twelve Scotch whiskies arranged in order of age, from oldest to youngest

VODKA AND OTHER NEUTRAL SPIRITS

CHAPTER THREE

LEARNING OBJECTIVES

After studying this chapter, the candidate should be able to do the following:

- Define vodka in terms of base materials, distillation processes, maturation, and other post-distillation procedures.
- Describe the main differences between American vodka and European vodka.

- Discuss the "flavored vodka" phenomenon.
- Recall and describe other neutral spirits, including high-proof neutral spirits, baijiu, shōchū, and soju.
- Discuss the sensory evaluation of vodka and the typical procedures for the serving of vodka and vodka-based drinks.

EXERCISE 1: DEFINITION AND HISTORY OF VODKA: MATCHING

Match each of the following terms with its appropriate definition. Each term will be used only once.

Grain	80°	Neutral spirits
Original vodka	Carbon	Grapes
60°	Stolichnaya	Potato
Smirnoff	75°	

1. _____ Element found in charcoal that is useful for filtration

2. _____ Minimum bottling proof for US vodka (unflavored)

3. _____ Minimum bottling proof for US flavored vodka

4. _____ Minimum bottling proof for EU vodka

5. _____ Considered to be the original base ingredient used for vodka

6. _____ Spirits produced from any material, distilled at or above 190 proof (per the US definition)

7. _____ A base material whose name must appear on the label if used for EU vodka

8. _____ The first brand of vodka to be produced in the United States

9. _____ Base ingredient used in the production of vodka after it was introduced to Europe from the New World

10. _____ The first brand of vodka to be imported into the United States from Russia

11. _____ Another term for unflavored vodka

EXERCISE 2: THE PRODUCTION OF VODKA

Mark each of the following statements as true or false.

1. _____ Fermentation of the base ingredients for vodka tends to be conducted quickly.

2. _____ The distillation process used in the production of vodka is designed to remove all congeners.

3. _____ Vodka produced in the United States is required to be distilled in a continuous column still.

4. _____ In the United States, vodka is required to be charcoal filtered after distillation.

5. _____ Vodka may be filtered using a variety of materials including crushed limestone, crushed industrial diamonds, and charcoal.

6. _____ EU vodka is considered a neutral spirit and is therefore not permitted to be aged longer than two months.

7. _____ American vodka has no required source of base ingredients and no required geographic area of production.

8. _____ US vodka is allowed to be bottled at a maximum of 40% alcohol by volume.

9. _____ One method of charcoal filtration used in the production of vodka allows the spirit to flow continuously through tanks of charcoal for a minimum of eight hours.

10. _____ Vodka produced in the United States is required to be distilled to a minimum of 190°.

11. _____ In the European Union, the use of pot stills is not permitted in the production of vodka.

12. _____ The type of water used in the production of vodka can have a large impact on the vodka's overall flavor profile.

13. _____ Many vodka producers use demineralized water in order to reduce unwanted flavors in the finished product.

14. _____ While most vodka is bottled unaged, aging is permitted.

15. _____ Grains and potatoes used in the production of vodka must undergo a conversion process before fermentation may begin.

EXERCISE 3: VODKA BY REGION: MATCHING

Match the following vodka brands by their country or region of production. Terms may be used more than once.

| Austria | United States | Sweden | The Netherlands | Canada |
| France | Poland | Russia | Finland | Iceland |

1. _____ Belvedere

2. _____ Grey Goose

3. _____ Tito's

4. _____ Ketel One

5. _____ Absolut

6. _____ Skyy

7. _____ Ikon

8. _____ Zytnia

9. _____ Iceberg

10. _____ Monopolowa

11. _____ Cîroc

12. _____ Ultimat

13. _____ Teton Glacier

14. _____ Wyborowa

15. _____ Luksusowa

16. _____ Charbay

17. _____ Chopin

18. _____ Stolichnaya

19. _____ Polstar

20. _____ Koskenforva

EXERCISE 4: FLAVORED VODKA: FILL IN THE BLANK/SHORT ANSWER

Fill in the blanks or provide a short answer for the following statements or questions.

1. _____ is an oak-aged vodka traditional to Poland and Lithuania.

2. _____ is a Polish term for vodka flavored with honey and herbs. It is often quite sweet and is sometimes served _____. This product is also made in Lithuania, where it is known as _____.

3. _____ is a Polish vodka flavored with bison grass. This type of product is also known in _____, where it goes by the name of Zubrovka.

4. _____ is a spicy-hot Russian vodka flavored with chili peppers. In order to reduce the impact of the heat, this vodka was often sweetened with _____.

5. Oak-aged vodka often has flavors such as vanilla, nutmeg, and smoke, which may be considered similar to some of the characteristics of _____.

6. _____ is a Russian product often known as "hunter's vodka." Hunter's vodka is flavored with a blend of spices, often led by the flavor of _____.

7. A unique bitter herb known as _____ is also part of the traditional recipe for hunter's vodka.

8. The minimum alcohol by volume for flavored vodka in the United States is _____.

9. In the United States, flavored vodka is sometimes cut with water to the minimum abv, prompting some brands to market themselves as a _____ alternative to original vodka.

10. In the European Union, the minimum alcohol by volume for flavored vodka is _____.

EXERCISE 5: VODKA AND NEUTRAL SPIRITS: FILL IN THE BLANK/SHORT ANSWER

Fill in the following chart with the missing information.

	Traditional base ingredient used for vodka production in Finland
	The flavor of American vodka is often compared to the flavor of this substance
	Traditional base ingredients used for vodka production in Poland
	American neutral spirit sometimes bottled as high as 190 proof and produced by the Luxco company
	Base materials that tend to produce vodka that is highly acidic and lighter in body
	Traditional base ingredient used for vodka production in Russia
	Base material that tends to produce vodka that is delicate in flavor and texture
	Flavor/texture characteristic found in some brands of vodka due to the presence of ethyl myristate and ethyl palmitate
	Brand of rectified spirit from Poland, often used to make homemade liqueurs
	Base materials that tend to produce vodka that is spicy and more robust in character
	Brand of neutral grain spirit produced in Germany, mostly for use in homemade liqueurs
	Base material that tends to produce vodka that is full-bodied and creamier on the palate
	Traditional base ingredient used for vodka production in Sweden
	Aromas found in some brands of vodka due to the presence of ethyl laurate

EXERCISE 6: BAIJIU, SHŌCHŪ, AND SOJU: MATCHING

Match each of the following terms with its appropriate definition. Each term will be used only once.

Japan	Qu	Wuliangye	Shaojiu
Korea	Jinro	Kōji	Komejōchū
China	Moutai	Imojōchū	Soba shōchū
Moromi	Erguotou	Kasutori shōchū	Mugijōchū

1. _____ Type of mold used to produce shōchū

2. _____ Country of origin for soju

3. _____ Buckwheat shōchū

4. _____ Type of baijiu bottled under the Red Star brand

5. _____ Rice shōchū

6. _____ Type of baijiu often known as "five grain drink"

7. _____ Country of origin for baijiu

8. _____ Barley shōchū

9. _____ Alternative name often used for baijiu

10. _____ Country of origin for shōchū

11. _____ The most widely distributed brand of soju

12. _____ Style of baijiu that was a favorite of Mao Zedong

13. _____ Sweet potato shōchū

14. _____ A bale or brick of grain filled with mold spores or yeast used in the production of baijiu

15. _____ Low-alcohol mash that is used in the production of shōchū

16. _____ Shōchū produced using the lees left over from the production of sake

1. Which of the following is true concerning vodka produced in the United States?
   a. US vodka may only be produced using a ferment made from grain or potatoes.
   b. US vodka must be distilled at or above 160 proof.
   c. US vodka and neutral spirits are the only American spirit categories required to be distilled at or above 190 proof.
   d. US vodka must be charcoal filtered either before or after distillation.

2. Which of the following countries is considered to be the first to produce vodka from potatoes?
   a. Russia
   b. Poland
   c. Finland
   d. Norway

3. What type of vodka is often referred to as *original vodka*?
   a. Unflavored vodka
   b. Charcoal-filtered vodka
   c. Polish vodka
   d. Vodka made using unmalted barley

4. What happened in the 1870s that led to improvements in the production and flavor of vodka?
   a. Rye was introduced to Poland and used exclusively in the production of vodka.
   b. The tsar nationalized the Russian vodka industry.
   c. Robert Stein invented the column still.
   d. The benefits of charcoal filtration were discovered.

5. Who is Rudolph Kunett?
   a. A former Russian who purchased the rights to produce vodka using the Smirnoff formula
   b. The inventor of the Moscow Mule
   c. The person who created Smirnoff's "It leaves you breathless" ad campaign
   d. The person who filed a lawsuit with the European Union concerning the use of grapes as a base ferment for EU vodka

6. Which of the following is true concerning EU vodka?
   a. EU vodka must be double distilled using a copper pot still
   b. EU vodka must be produced via continuous distillation in a column still
   d. EU vodka must be charcoal filtered after distillation
   d. EU vodka must be bottled at a minimum of 37.5% abv

7. The vodkas of Finland have traditionally been produced using which of the following base materials?
   a. Potatoes
   b. Winter wheat
   c. Barley
   d. Grapes

8. Which of the following is an oak-aged vodka traditional to Poland and Lithuania?
   a. Zubrówka
   b. Starka
   c. Okhotnichya
   d. Krupnik

9. What is the required minimum alcohol content for US flavored vodka?
   a. 30% abv
   b. 35% abv
   c. 37.5% abv
   d. 40% abv

10. Which of the following is used as the typical base ingredient for Cîroc vodka?
    a. Grapes
    b. Winter wheat
    c. Rye
    d. Potatoes

11. Which of the following is used to flavor Kubanskaya?
    a. Bison grass
    b. Red chili pepper
    c. Dried orange peels
    d. Smoked salt

12. Which of the following is a Chinese spirit often produced with sorghum?
    a. Soju
    b. Koji
    c. Jinro
    d. Baijiu

28

CHAPTER FOUR GIN AND OTHER FLAVORED SPIRITS

GIN AND OTHER FLAVORED SPIRITS

LEARNING OBJECTIVES

After studying this chapter, the candidate should be able to do the following:

- Define gin in terms of base materials, distillation processes, maturation, and other post-distillation procedures.
- Identify the various botanicals used in the production of gin.
- Define the London dry, Plymouth, and Old Tom styles of gin.

- Describe the various juniper-flavored spirit drinks, including Steinhäger, genever, and wacholder.
- Identify and discuss the various anise-flavored spirits, such as raki, absinthe, Pernod, pastis, and ouzo.
- Identify and discuss other flavored spirits including pacharán and akvavit.
- Discuss the sensory evaluation of gin and the typical procedures for the serving of gin and gin-based drinks.

EXERCISE 1: THE DEFINITION OF GIN: TRUE OR FALSE

Mark each of the following statements as true or false.

1. _____ Gin produced in the European Union must be bottled at a minimum of 35% abv.

2. _____ Compound gin may be produced by combining neutral spirits with juniper extract.

3. _____ Gin may be produced in the United States via the mixing of neutral spirits and botanical extracts.

4. _____ According to the standards of the European Union, genever is a type of gin.

5. _____ All types of gin must be flavored with juniper.

6. _____ Gin produced in the United States must be bottled at a minimum of 80 proof.

7. _____ According to EU standards, London dry gin must be produced in London.

8. _____ Old Tom gin may be produced in the United States.

9. _____ In the European Union, London dry gin may contain a maximum of 10 grams of sugar per liter.

10. _____ In the EU, Steinhäger is considered a type of juniper-flavored spirit as opposed to a true gin.

EXERCISE 2: BOTANICALS: MATCHING

Match each of the following terms with its appropriate definition. Terms may be used more than once.

Gentian   Coriander seed   Juniper
Cardamom   Angelica   Calamus
Orris root   Quinine
Hyssop   Cassia

1. _____   The second most widely used botanical for the flavoring of gin

2. _____   The seedpods of a variety of plants in the ginger family

3. _____   Provides an aroma similar to violets

4. _____   The root of a plant with trumpet-shaped flowers

5. _____   Occurs naturally in the bark of the cinchona tree

6. _____   Often used as a substitute for ginger, nutmeg, or cinnamon

7. _____   The seed of a plant also known as Chinese parsley

8. _____   The berries of an evergreen tree

9. _____   A flowering plant also known as "sweet flag"

10. _____   Provides a minty aroma and flavor, is somewhat bitter, and is also used in herbal medicine

11. _____   An herb that is often candied and used as a culinary decoration

12. _____   A spice related to "true" Sri Lanka cinnamon

EXERCISE 3: METHODS OF GIN PRODUCTION: COMPARISON

For each of the following statements, determine whether it is true concerning the production of gin made using original distillation, redistillation, cold compounding, and/or the essential oils technique. Place a check mark in the column of every production process that is accurately described by the corresponding statement.

Statement	Original Distillation	Redistillation	Cold Compounding	Essential Oils
1. Uses fermented mash				
2. Uses neutral spirits and botanicals enclosed in a mesh bag				
3. When done in altered air pressure, may be referred to as vacuum distillation				
4. Produces a style of gin considered to be lower quality than distilled gin				
5. Also known as the compounding essence procedure				
6. Uses a specialized still with a gin head				
7. Involves "soaking" neutral spirits with a batch of crushed botanicals				
8. Also known as direct distillation				
9. Produces a style of gin known as compound gin				
10. Uses neutral spirits				

Fill in the blanks or provide a short answer for the following statements or questions.

1. _____ is the only additive allowed to be added to London dry gin after distillation.

2. According to EU standards, London dry gin must have less than _____ of sugar per liter.

3. The style of London dry gin is described as _____, with a clean juniper berry flavor.

4. Plymouth gin was first produced in the year _____.

5. The building that houses the Plymouth Distillery used to be a Dominican monastery inhabited by an order known as the _____.

6. _____ is a PGI gin from Lithuania.

7. In 1896, Plymouth gin was mentioned in a recipe for a drink known as the Marguerite Cocktail, which would later become known as the _____.

8. The _____ ship is part of the trademark label of Plymouth gin.

9. Hayman Distillery in _____ and Ransom Spirits in _____ are two of the modern producers of Old Tom gin.

10. _____ was the original gin used in the Tom Collins cocktail.

11. According to legend, a London merchant named _____ sold gin from his house, via a dispenser shaped like a black cat.

12. The specialized type of still that contains a perforated gin head was originally known as a _____ still.

13. Flavored gin produced in the United States must be bottled at a minimum of _____ alcohol by volume.

14. Gin de Mahón is a PGI gin produced on the Spanish island of _____.

EXERCISE 5: JUNIPER-FLAVORED SPIRIT DRINKS

Match each of the following terms with its appropriate definition. Terms may be used more than once.

Belgium   Oude   Wacholder
France   Koptstootjes   Steinhäger
Germany   Holland gin
Jonge   Genever

1. _____   Spirit produced at the Eversbusch Distillery since 1817

2. _____   Country of production for Hasseltse Jenever

3. _____   Another name for genever

4. _____   A style of genever that must contain a minimum of 15% malt spirit

5. _____   A spirit that was awarded a PGI in 2008

6. _____   Country of production for Genièvre Flandres Artois

7. _____   The H. W. Schlichte Company is the oldest producer of this spirit

8. _____   Country of production for wacholder

9. _____   A spirit that was awarded a PGI in 1989

10. _____   The German word for *juniper*

11. _____   Country of production for Steinhäger

12. _____   A type of genever that may not contain more than 15% malt spirit

13. _____   A customary method of service for genever

14. _____   Term often used in Germany for all juniper-flavored spirit drinks

EXERCISE 6: FLAVORED SPIRITS: FILL IN THE BLANK/SHORT ANSWER

Fill in the following chart with the missing information.

	Location of first absinthe distillery
	Chemical compound often blamed for certain (alleged) harmful effects of the consumption of absinthe
	Year that absinthe became legal in the United States (after a ninety-year ban)
	Country of origin for the unsweetened anise-flavored spirit known as raki
	Base material which is fermented and used in the production of high-quality raki
	The base spirit that will be redistilled and made into raki
	Product launched in 1928 as a sweeter alternative to absinthe, "minus the wormwood"
	Dry, anise-flavored spirit launched by Paul Ricard in the 1930s
	The leading anise-flavored spirit in Greece
	Sloe berry–flavored liqueur made with anise-flavored spirits, popular in Spain's Basque Country
	Main flavoring in akvavit
	Term used to indicate a clear, unaged (or just slightly aged) style of akvavit
	Style of akvavit that is aged based on a unique tradition of sailing ships
	Country that has PGI status for akvavit
	French product with PGI status for absinthe

1. What is the minimum level of alcohol required for gin produced in the European Union?
   a. 35% abv
   b. 37% abv
   c. 37.5% abv
   d. 40% abv

2. During which time period was the "gin craze" at its height?
   a. 1680–1700
   b. 1720–1750
   c. 1775–1800
   d. 1800–1830

3. Which of the following gin botanicals are all part of the "bark" category?
   a. Fennel, ginger, and gentian
   b. Cassia, cinnamon, and quinine
   c. Calamus, angelica, and coriander
   d. Vanilla, clove, and quinine

4. Which of the following processes is used to produce compound gin?
   a. The essential oils method
   b. Original distillation
   c. Vacuum distillation
   d. Cold distillation

5. Which of the following methods is used to produce Sacred Gin?
   a. The circulatory method
   b. Cold compounding
   c. The compounding essence procedure
   d. Vacuum distillation

6. Which of the following types of gin was originally produced at the former Black Friars Distillery?
   a. London dry gin
   b. Plymouth gin
   c. Oxley gin
   d. Genever gin

7. Flavored gins produced in the United States must be bottled at what minimum level of alcohol?
   a. 30% abv
   b. 35% abv
   c. 37.5% abv
   d. 40% abv

8. What is genever?
   a. A type of flavored gin
   b. A type of juniper-flavored spirit drink
   c. A gin-based liqueur
   d. An anise-flavored spirit drink

9. What is the aging requirement for "oude" genever?
   a. It is not required to be aged
   b. Six months in oak
   c. Six months in any type of container
   d. One year in oak

10. What is the base material used in the production of high-quality raki?
    a. Malted grain
    b. Unmalted barley
    c. Sultana grapes
    d. Potatoes

11. Which of the following chemicals was once blamed for many alleged harmful effects of absinthe?
    a. Thujone
    b. Sulfites
    c. Thymol
    d. Formaldehyde

12. Which of the following products has PGI status?
    a. London dry gin
    b. Pacharán Navarro
    c. Old Tom gin
    d. Plymouth gin

WHISKEY

LEARNING OBJECTIVES

After studying this chapter, the candidate should be able to do the following:
- Define whiskey in terms of base materials, distillation processes, maturation, and other post-distillation procedures.
- Describe the various types of whiskey, including Scotch whisky, Irish whiskey, bourbon, Tennessee whiskey, Canadian whisky, and Japanese whisky.

- Identify and discuss the various types of American whiskey, including corn whiskey, rye whiskey, straight whiskey, and bottled-in-bond.
- Describe the product category known as white whiskeys.
- Discuss the sensory evaluation of whiskey and the typical procedures for the serving of whiskey and whiskey-based drinks.

EXERCISE 1: THE DEFINITION OF WHISKEY: TRUE OR FALSE

Mark each of the following statements as true or false.

1. _True_   In the United States, whiskey must be distilled at less than 95% abv.

2. _____ Bourbon whiskey must be produced from a mash of at least 51% corn.

3. _____ All European rye whiskey may be released after a minimum of two years of oak aging.

4. _____ Straight bourbon whiskey must be aged for a minimum of four years in oak.

5. _____ Both EU and American whiskey must be bottled at a minimum of 40% abv.

6. _____ American corn whiskey does not have to be stored in oak, but if it is, the barrels must be used or uncharred wood.

7. _____ All American wheat whiskeys must be aged for a minimum of two years in oak.

8. _____ EU whiskey must be distilled to less than 94.8% abv.

9. _____ American rye whiskey must be made from a mash containing a minimum of 80% malted or unmalted rye.

10. _____ American corn whiskey must be made from a mash containing a minimum of 80% corn.

11. _____ There is no requirement for American wheat whiskey to be stored in oak containers.

12. _____ The minimum aging for both Irish whiskey and Scotch whisky is three years in oak.

EXERCISE 2: WHISKEY PRODUCTION (FERMENTATION AND DISTILLATION): MATCHING

Match each of the following terms with its appropriate definition. Terms may be used more than once.

Wort   Mash cooker   Kilning
Sodium   Mash tun   Green malt
Iron   Maltose   Grain bill
Grist   Malting   Mashing
Fermentation   Wash

1. _____   European term for the vessel used for mixing ground malt with hot water

2. _____   The stage where germination of the grain is stopped

3. _____   The sugary liquid that is drained away from the ground grain

4. _____   In Scotland, this process may occur in a washback

5. _____   In this stage of production, enzymes complete the starch conversion process

6. _____   Type of sugar that is produced when grain is soaked in water

7. _____   If used to produce whiskey, water that contains high levels of this mineral can give the spirit a black hue

8. _____   The list of ingredients that will be fermented for a particular type of whiskey

9. _____   Mineral found in soft water

10. _____   Stage of whiskey production during which grain is soaked in water

11. _____   Term used for roasted, ground grain

12. _____   Term used for the fermented liquid that is ready to be distilled

13. _____   Term used for malted barley or grain

14. _____   In the United States, this vessel may be used for mixing ground malt with hot water

15. _____   The stage where peat may be used

EXERCISE 3: WHISKEY: TIME LINE

Put the following stages of whiskey production into typical chronological order, starting with the selection of the grain bill and following through the production process. Note that some of these procedures are optional and are, therefore, not always used in the production of some types of whiskey. The first answer has been provided for you.

Blending   Grain bill   Mashing
Bottling   Green malt   Maturation
Distillation in a wash still   Kilning   Milling
Distillation in a spirit still   Low wines   New-make spirit
Fermentation   Malting   Washing

1. Grain bill _____

2. _____

3. _____

4. _____

5. _____

6. _____

7. _____

8. _____

9. _____

10. _____

11. _____

12. _____

13. _____

14. _____

15. _____

EXERCISE 4: WHISKEY PRODUCTION (MATURATION AND BOTTLING): TRUE OR FALSE

Mark each of the following statements as true or false.

1. _____ Contact with the red layer of an oak barrel darkens the color of a spirit.

2. _____ During the process of oak aging, oxidation will cause the color of the spirit to lighten.

3. _____ The greater the diurnal temperature swing, the greater the effect of maturation.

4. _____ Whisky-aging warehouses in northern Europe tend to be one-story stone buildings.

5. _____ In general, Tennessee whiskey requires a longer aging period than Scotch whisky in order to achieve the same results.

6. _____ Rackhouses are typically several stories high, with wide temperature fluctuations between the top and bottom floors.

7. _____ American distillers are more likely to use new oak barrels for whiskey maturation than are European distillers.

8. _____ Single-barrel bottlings are by far the largest category of whisky, according to global sales (by volume).

9. _____ No water is added during the bottling process to a whisky that is labeled with the term *cask-strength*.

10. _____ Almost all whiskey is a blend of sorts, crafted from multiple barrels of a single product.

11. _____ Both water and alcohol will evaporate through the pores of a barrel.

12. _____ Most whisky distilleries in northern Europe use new oak barrels to age their whiskies.

13. _____ Multi-story rackhouses are commonly used to age whiskey throughout Ireland and Scotland.

14. _____ Some experts estimate that it takes over three years of aging whisky in Scotland to achieve the same results that are achieved in Kentucky in a single year.

15. _____ As the outside temperature lowers and cools the spirit, the spirit expands and is forced into the barrel staves.

EXERCISE 5: SCOTCH WHISKY: MATCHING

Match each of the following terms with its appropriate definition. Terms may be used more than once.

Blended Scotch	Blended grain Scotch	The Highlands
Single malt Scotch	Malted barley	Islay
Blended malt Scotch	Wheat	The Lowlands
Single grain Scotch	Campbeltown	Speyside

1. _____ A whisky produced from the single malt Scotch whiskies of two or more distilleries

2. _____ At least a portion must be used in all types of Scotch

3. _____ A blend of one or more single grain Scotch whiskies with one or more single malt Scotch whiskies

4. _____ Must be produced at a single distillery from 100% malted barley and no other grains

5. _____ Region that includes the islands of Mull, Jura, and Skye

6. _____ Declared a separate whisky-producing region as of 2009

7. _____ A Scotch whisky distilled at a single distillery from malted barley and other grains

8. _____ An ingredient that may be used in single grain Scotch but not in single malt Scotch

9. _____ A whisky produced from the single grain Scotch whiskies of two or more distilleries

10. _____ Accounts for over 90% of the Scotch whisky consumed worldwide

11. _____ Considered to be the premium product among the five categories of Scotch whisky

12. _____ Region known for producing whiskies with a medium to strong peat character

13. _____ Region traditionally known for a lighter style of whisky produced via triple distillation

14. _____ Region that has the largest number of operating distilleries in Scotland

15. _____ Region located on Scotland's Kintyre Peninsula

Using the diagram and the place-names listed below, identify the whisky-producing areas of Scotland.

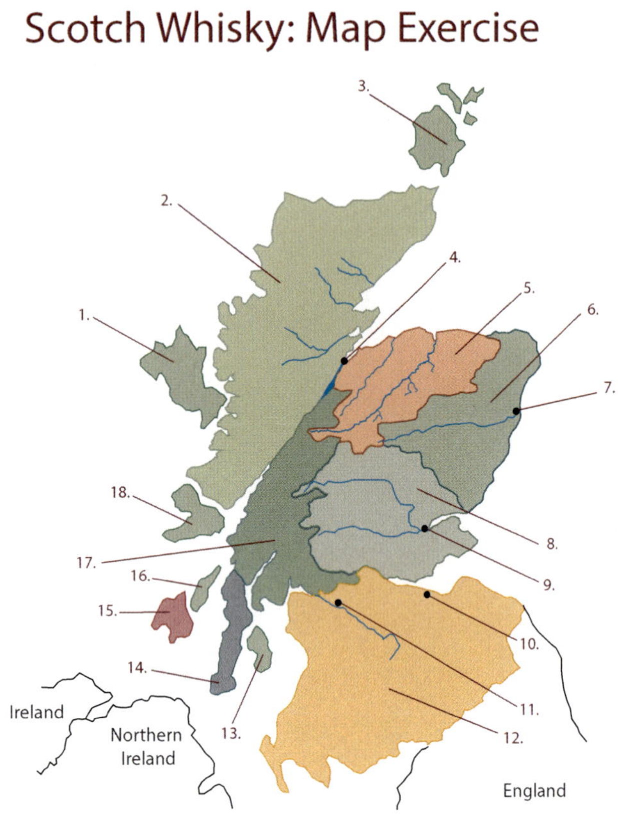

Scotch Whisky: Map Exercise

Figure 5.1: Scotch Whisky Map Exercise

Isle of Arran	Northern Highlands
Perth	Lowlands
Aberdeen	Central Highlands
Glasgow	Campbeltown
Islay	Isle of Skye
Inverness	Speyside
Isle of Mull	Western Highlands
Eastern Highlands	Orkney Islands
Edinburgh	Isle of Jura

1. _____

2. _____

3. _____

4. _____

5. _____

6. _____

7. _____

8. _____

9. _____

10. _____

11. _____

12. _____

13. _____

14. _____

15. _____

16. _____

17. _____

18. _____

For each of the following statements concerning Irish whiskey, determine whether it is true of Irish malt whiskey, Irish grain whiskey, Irish pot still whiskey, and/or blended Irish whiskey. Place a check mark in the column of every style of whiskey to which the statement applies.

Statement	Irish Malt Whiskey	Irish Grain Whiskey	Irish Pot Still Whiskey	Blended Irish Whiskey
1. Must be distilled using pot stills				
2. Must be bottled in Ireland or shipped off the island in inert bulk containers				
3. May be produced using double or triple distillation				
4. Must be made using 100% malted barley				
5. Must be produced using a maximum of 30% malted barley				
6. Must be produced using a minimum of 30% of both malted and unmalted barley				
7. Often contains up to 5% oats or rye				
8. Not allowed to be exported in any type of wooden container				
9. Produced using two or more different whiskey types				
10. Must be stored in wooden casks not to exceed 700 liters in capacity for at least three years				
11. Produced using a mixture of malted and unmalted grains				

EXERCISE 8: EUROPEAN WHISKEY: TRUE OR FALSE

Mark each of the following statements as true or false.

1. _____ Scotch whisky and Irish whiskey are both required to be distilled at no more than 94.8% abv.

2. _____ A whiskey known as Redbreast is produced at the New Midleton Distillery.

3. _____ As of October 2015, a new set of technical standards was implemented for the production of Scotch whisky.

4. _____ Irish distilleries may use new or used oak barrels for the maturation of whiskey.

5. _____ Blended Irish whiskey often has a "leathery" flavor due to the use of unmalted grains.

6. _____ Irish malt whiskey is required to be aged for a minimum of eight years in oak.

7. _____ Scotch whisky and Irish whiskey are both required to be aged in oak casks for a minimum of three years.

8. _____ There are currently more than one hundred whiskey distilleries operating in Ireland.

9. _____ If solids from the milling and mashing stages remain in the wort during fermentation, a more malty-flavored spirit will result.

10. _____ The aroma known as *peat reek* is more likely to be found in Scotch whiskies than in Irish whiskeys.

11. _____ Most Scotch grain whisky is very full-flavored and likely to be distilled in a copper pot still.

12. _____ All Irish whiskey is triple-distilled.

13. _____ Glen Scotia distillery is located in Scotland's Campbeltown region.

14. _____ In general, Irish whiskey is considered to be smoother and less "smoky" than Scotch.

15. _____ Caramel coloring is not allowed to be used as an additive in single grain Scotch whisky.

EXERCISE 9: BOURBON WHISKEY: FILL IN THE BLANK/SHORT ANSWER

Fill in the blanks or provide a short answer for the following statements or questions.

1. Bourbon is required to be made from at least 51% _____, but many high-quality bourbons contain as much as _____.

2. Bourbon must be distilled at an alcohol level not to exceed _____ proof.

3. During the distillation of bourbon, some residue from the first distillation run, known as _____, may be placed back in the fermenter for use in the next batch. This process is known as _____.

4. Typically, the first distillation of bourbon is done is pot stills or single column stills known as _____. The second distillation takes place in a _____ or a thumper.

5. A thumper uses heated water to capture and drain off the _____ of the distillation run.

6. Bourbon must be stored at not more than _____ in _____ new oak containers.

7. In the year _____, the US Congress passed a resolution declaring that bourbon is a _____ product of the United States.

8. Most bourbon is blended before bottling, but sometimes the best barrels, known as _____, may be bottled as single-barrel bourbon.

9. Bourbon that is labeled as _____ may contain coloring, flavoring, or other spirits, but it must be at least _____ straight bourbon.

10. While bourbon may be produced anywhere in the United States, 95% of all bourbon is produced in _____.

11. Bourbon that has been aged for at least two years in charred new oak containers may be labeled as _____.

Fill in the following chart with the missing information.

	Tennessee whiskey must undergo this charcoal-filtering process
	Tennessee distillery that was granted an exception to the charcoal-filtering rule
	Brand of American rye whiskey founded in 1810
	Aging requirement for American corn whiskey
	The six types of American straight whiskeys
	Minimum aging requirement for American straight whiskeys that have an age statement on the label
	Minimum aging requirement for American straight whiskeys that do not have an age statement on the label
	Required bottling proof for American bottled-in-bond whiskey
	A mixture of neutral spirits mixed with no less than 5% whiskey
	Another term for Jacob's Ghost or other types of white whiskey
	Obscure whiskey product that must be distilled to higher than 160 proof but lower than 190 proof

EXERCISE 11: CANADIAN WHISKY: TRUE OR FALSE

Mark each of the following statements as true or false.

1. _____ Canadian whisky is required to be aged for a minimum of two years in small wooden containers.

2. _____ Canadian grain whisky is sometimes referred to as base whisky.

3. _____ Specific styles of Canadian whisky, such as those produced using a large amount of rye or those stored in charred oak barrels, are often referred to as flavoring whiskies.

4. _____ Glenora Distillery is located in Ontario.

5. _____ Canadian blended whisky may contain up to 9.09% additives, which may include wine, sweetener, brandy, and/or caramel coloring.

6. _____ All of the products in Canadian blended whisky—including base whisky, flavoring whisky, and other additives—must be of Canadian origin.

7. _____ Stalk and Barrel single malt whisky is produced in British Columbia.

8. _____ In terms of volume, the largest production of Canadian whisky is single malt whisky.

9. _____ Most Canadian blended whiskies are produced using grain whisky and flavoring whisky.

10. _____ A good deal of Canadian base whisky is made using wheat or corn as the main ingredient.

11. _____ Canadian whisky labeled with the term *rye whisky* must be produced using a minimum of 51% rye.

12. _____ Canadian grain whisky is not typically bottled and labeled as such, but rather is used to produce Canadian blended whisky.

13. _____ Canadian single malt whisky is required to be aged in small wooden containers for a minimum of four years.

14. _____ Canadian blended whisky is permitted to contain small amounts of sherry.

15. _____ During American Prohibition, large amounts of Canadian whisky were smuggled into the United States.

EXERCISE 12: INTERNATIONAL WHISKIES: MATCHING

Match each of the following terms with its appropriate definition. Terms may be used more than once.

Suntory Distillery
Hazelburn Distillery
Amrut Distilleries
Brilliance
Whisky DYC

Yamazaki
Yoichi Distillery
Tasmania Distillery
Officer's Choice
Feni

Southern Distilleries
Pradlo Distillery
Miyagikyo

1. _____   A distillery operated by Nikka Whisky and located on the island of Hokkaido

2. _____   The first producer of a true grain-based whisky in India

3. _____   A distillery in the Czech Republic

4. _____   Producer of Sullivans Cove Single Cask Malt Whisky

5. _____   Producer of New Zealand's Hokonui Moonshine

6. _____   The first commercial whisky distillery in Japan

7. _____   A popular style of molasses-based "whisky" produced in India

8. _____   A 100% grain-based whisky produced in India by John Distilleries

9. _____   Distillery operated by Nikka Whisky and located in the city of Sendai

10. _____   An Indian spirit distilled from cashew fruit

11. _____   Scotland distillery where Masataka Taketsuru trained

12. _____   Original location of Japan's first whisky distillery

13. _____   Producer of Hammer Head whisky

14. _____   Large producer of Spanish whisky

EXERCISE 13: WHISKEY: BRANDS

Using the following list of whiskeys, place each under the appropriate column based on the country of origin.

Ardbeg	Dalwhinnie	Jack Daniel's	Old Overholt
Ballantine's	Dewar's	Jameson	Redbreast
Benjamin Prichard's	Echlinville	Jim Beam	Talisker
Buffalo Trace	Famous Grouse	Johnnie Walker	Teeling
Chivas Regal	Four Roses	Kilbeggan	Tullamore D.E.W.
Cooley	Glenlivet	Macallan	West Cork
Connemara	Glenora	Maker's Mark	Wild Turkey
Crown Royal	George Dickel	Midleton	William Peel
Cutty Sark	Green Spot	Old Bushmills	Woodford Reserve
Dalmore	J&B	Old Forester	

Scotland	Ireland	United States	Canada

1. American rye whiskey must be distilled at an alcohol by volume not to exceed:
   a. 190 proof
   b. 180 proof
   c. 160 proof
   d. 150 proof

2. EU whiskey must be stored for no less than three years in wooden casks with a maximum volume of:
   a. 1,000 liters/265 gallons
   b. 700 liters/185 gallons
   c. 500 liters/132 gallons
   d. 250 liters/66 gallons

3. Of the following grains, which is considered to be the best source for the enzymes that will help to convert the grain's starch to a fermentable form of sugar?
   a. Barley
   b. Wheat
   c. Corn
   d. Rye

4. Which of the following is a well-known brand of Scotch whisky?
   a. Connemara
   b. Evan Williams
   c. Jack Daniel's
   d. Johnnie Walker

5. During which of the following whiskey-producing procedures is the wort separated from the grain?
   a. Kilning
   b. Malting
   c. Washing
   d. Milling

6. Which of the following products comes off the spirit still?
   a. Low wines
   b. High wines
   c. Mash
   d. High beers

7. Which of the following is one of the five categories of Scotch whisky, as defined by the Scotch Whisky Regulations?
   a. Single grain Scotch whisky
   b. Pure malt Scotch whisky
   c. Vatted malt Scotch whisky
   d. Single blend Scotch whisky

8. Which of the following processes of Scotch production is most likely to involve the use of peat?
   a. Malting
   b. Mashing
   c. Fermentation
   d. Kilning

9. Which of the following brands of Scotch is produced in the Highlands region?
   a. Ardbeg
   b. The Glenlivet
   c. Dalmore
   d. Bladnoch

10. Which of the following brands of Scotch is produced in Islay?
    a. Dalwhinnie
    b. Glenkinchie
    c. Glenmorangie
    d. Laphroaig

11. Irish whiskey must be distilled to an alcoholic strength of less than:
    a. 160.2 proof
    b. 180.8 proof
    c. 189.6 proof
    d. 190.2 proof

12. Irish pot still whiskey must contain what minimum amount of malted barley?
    a. 20%
    b. 30%
    c. 50%
    d. 51%

13. Which American statesman created the Bottled-in-Bond Act of 1897?
    a. E. H. Taylor
    b. George Garvin Brown
    c. Bill Haslam
    d. Grover Cleveland

14. Which of the following products is most likely to have undergone the Lincoln County Process?
    a. Jack Daniel's
    b. Benjamin Prichard's
    c. Jim Beam
    d. Four Roses

15. Which of the following products may contain up to 9.09% additives, including wine, sherry, and caramel coloring?
    a. Canadian grain whisky
    b. Canadian blended whisky
    c. American light whiskey
    d. Bourbon

16. What is Green Spot?
    a. Bourbon
    b. Tennessee whiskey
    c. Irish pot still whiskey
    d. Indian whisky

17. Which of the following areas is located farthest south?
    a. The Orkney Islands
    b. Speyside
    c. The Isle of Mull
    d. The Eastern Highlands

18. Where is Sullivans Cove Single Cask Malt Whisky produced?
    a. Scotland
    b. Australia
    c. New Zealand
    d. Ireland

19. Which of the following is a 100% grain-based whisky produced in India?
    a. Amrut
    b. Royal Stag
    c. Shirofuda White Label
    d. Hokonui Moonshine

20. Which of the following products does not need to be stored in wood barrels?
    a. Blended Scotch whisky
    b. Straight bourbon
    c. Irish pot still whiskey
    d. American corn whiskey

BRANDY AND OTHER FRUIT-BASED SPIRITS

LEARNING OBJECTIVES

After studying this chapter, the candidate should be able to do the following:

- Define brandy in terms of base materials, distillation processes, maturation, and other post-distillation procedures.
- Describe the various types of grape-based brandy, including cognac, armagnac, brandy de Jerez, pisco, and other grape brandies produced throughout the world.

- Identify and discuss the various types of pomace brandy, including grappa and marc.
- Discuss the various types of apple- and pear-based brandy, including calvados and applejack. Identify and define other fruit-based brandies, fruit-based spirits, and flavored brandies.
- Discuss the sensory evaluation of brandy and the typical procedures for the serving of brandy and brandy-based drinks.

EXERCISE 1: THE DEFINITION OF BRANDY: TRUE OR FALSE

Mark each of the following statements as true or false.

1. _____ In the United States, a product labeled as "brandy" must be produced solely from grapes (which may contain up to 30% grape pomace or lees).

2. _____ EU brandy made using Bartlett pears may be labeled as "Williams."

3. _____ In the United States, "neutral brandy" must be distilled at a minimum of 190 proof.

4. _____ EU brandy must be aged for at least one year in any type of oak container, or for at least six months in small oak barrels.

5. _____ Kirschwasser is a type of fruit spirit produced in the European Union.

6. _____ Both US and EU brandy must be bottled at a minimum of 40% abv.

7. _____ Fruit brandy produced in the European Union is technically classified as a "fruit spirit."

8. _____ In the United States, the term *applejack* is synonymous with "apple brandy."

9. _____ Plum-based spirits produced in the European Union must be aged for at least one year in wood.

10. _____ In the United States, a product labeled as "brandy" must have been aged for at least two years in wood.

11. _____ In the United States, pomace brandy must be aged for a minimum of one year.

12. _____ In the European Union, the term *weinbrand* may be used only for a certain type of plum brandy.

Match each of the following terms with its appropriate definition. Each term will be used only once.

Hennessy   Bois Ordinaires   Folignan
Rémy Martin   Martell   Bon Bois
Grande Champagne   Première chauffe   Bonne chauffe
Saint-Émilion   Brouillis   À repasse
Boisé   Ugni Blanc   Petite Champagne

1. _____   A name for the two-stage cognac distillation process

2. _____   Subregion of Cognac with predominantly clay soils

3. _____   The distillate produced by the first stage of cognac distillation

4. _____   Cognac house that pioneered the production method that discards the lees left over after fermentation

5. _____   The largest of the two most prestigious crus of Cognac

6. _____   A type of oak extract allowed for use in Cognac

7. _____   Name used throughout most of France for the leading grape variety used in cognac

8. _____   Cognac house that pioneered the production method that reuses the lees in order to impart a richer character to the spirit

9. _____   Local name for the Ugni Blanc grape variety used in the Cognac region

10. _____   Considered to be the most prestigious of the six subregions of Cognac

11. _____   The first stage of cognac distillation

12. _____   A grape approved for use in cognac, but limited to a maximum of 10% of all plantings

13. _____   The second stage of cognac distillation

14. _____   The top-selling cognac brand (by global sales)

15. _____   Subregion of Cognac with mostly sandy soils

EXERCISE 3: THE COGNAC REGION: MAP EXERCISE

Using the diagram and the place-names listed below, identify the regions and cities within the cognac-producing region. Some place-names may be used more than once.

Cognac: Map Exercise

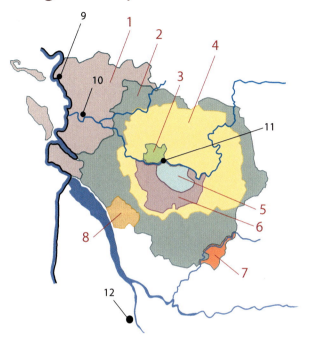

Copyright: The Society of Wine Educators 2015

Figure 6.1: Cognac Map Exercise

Bois Ordinaires
Bons Bois
Borderies
City of Bordeaux
City of Cognac
Fins Bois
Grande Champagne
La Rochelle
Petite Champagne
Rochefort

1. _____

2. _____

3. _____

4. _____

5. _____

6. _____

7. _____

8. _____

9. _____

10. _____

11. _____

12. _____

Fill in the following chart with the missing information.

	The full, official name of cognac
	Labeling term used to indicate a cognac produced with a combination of grapes from the Grande Champagne and Petite Champagne areas (with at least 50% from Grande Champagne)
	Labeling terms used for cognac with a minimum of two years of wood aging
	Labeling term used for cognac with a minimum of three years of wood aging
	Labeling terms used for cognac with a minimum of four years of wood aging
	Labeling terms used for cognac with a minimum of five years of wood aging
	Labeling terms used for cognac with a minimum of six years of wood aging
	Labeling term used for cognac with a minimum of ten years of wood aging
	Labeling term that translates as "beyond age"
	Agency that oversees the inventory and age control of cognac
	French term for the "golden certificate" that must accompany every consignment of cognac

EXERCISE 5: ARMAGNAC: MATCHING

Match each of the following terms with its appropriate definition. Terms may be used more than once.

Mauzac	Blanche	Folle Blanche
Baco Blanc	Floc de Gascogne	Boulbènes
Ugni Blanc	Monlezun	Bas-Armagnac
Haut-Armagnac	Vintage	
Clairette de Gascogne	Colombard	

1. _____ A type of armagnac produced from the grapes of a single year's harvest

2. _____ Minor grape variety of armagnac, also known as Blanc Dame

3. _____ A forest located close to the Armagnac region that produces highly tannic oak

4. _____ A type of topsoil found in the Bas-Armagnac consisting of sand, chalk, clay, and stones

5. _____ Category of armagnac that may be released after three months of aging

6. _____ Minor grape of the Armagnac region, allowed in both Blanc and Rosé sub-varieties

7. _____ A sweet wine made in the Haut-Armagnac area

8. _____ Type of oak often used for the first year of the aging of armagnac

9. _____ Grape that accounts for nearly 60% of the Armagnac vineyards

10. _____ Grape used to add a spicy, peppery edge to armagnac

11. _____ Considered to be the highest-quality subregion of Armagnac

12. _____ A hybrid grape used in the production of armagnac

13. _____ Subregion known for producing the lightest-styled spirits of the Armagnac area

14. _____ Grape used to add a floral aroma and subtlety to armagnac

Using the diagram and the place-names listed below, identify the regions and cities within the armagnac-producing region.

Armagnac: Map Exercise

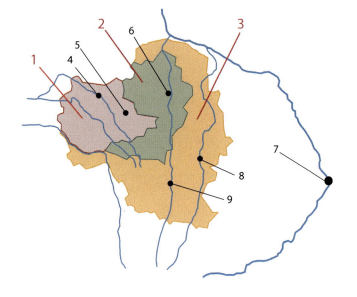

Copyright: The Society of Wine Educators 2015

1. _____

2. _____

3. _____

4. _____

5. _____

6. _____

7. _____

8. _____

9. _____

Figure 6.2: Armagnac Map Exercise

Auch
Bas-Armagnac
Cazaubon
Condom
Eauze
Haut-Armagnac
Mirande
Ténarèze
Toulouse

EXERCISE 7: BRANDY DE JEREZ: FILL IN THE BLANK/SHORT ANSWER

Fill in the following chart with the missing information.

	Area where most of the grapes for brandy de Jerez are grown
	Variety that provides 95% of the grapes for brandy de Jerez
	Variety that provides 5% of the grapes for brandy de Jerez
	The three towns that make up the "Sherry Triangle" within the Brandy de Jerez PGI
	Base spirit that has up to 70% abv
	Base spirit that has up to 80% abv
	Base spirit that has up to 94.8% abv
	Specialized stills used to produce high-quality brandy de Jerez
	Series of barrels used for aging brandy de Jerez
	Labeling term used for brandy de Jerez that has a minimum of six months of solera aging in wood
	Labeling term used for brandy de Jerez that has a minimum of one year of solera aging in wood
	Labeling term used for 100% holandas brandy de Jerez that has a minimum of three years of solera aging in wood

Mark each of the following statements as true or false.

1. _____ In 2013, the European Union recognized the Chilean province of Pisco as being the geographical origin of pisco.

2. _____ The Peruvian version of the Pisco Sour is traditionally shaken with egg whites and served with a dash of Angostura bitters.

3. _____ The Elqui Valley, a subregion of the Coquimbo region, is the leading area for the production of Chilean pisco.

4. _____ Pisco corriente, produced in Chile, must be a minimum of 43% abv.

5. _____ Pisco envejecido is an aged pisco produced in Chile.

6. _____ While often assumed to be a pomace brandy, most high-quality pisco is produced from fermented grape must.

7. _____ According to both the United States and the European Union, Chile and Peru are the only two countries allowed to produce a product named pisco.

8. _____ Aromatic grape varieties used in the production of Peruvian pisco include Italia, Moscatel, and Albilla.

9. _____ The United States recognizes Pisco Perú as a distinctive product of Peru, but has not yet recognized Pisco Chileno as a distinctive product of Chile.

10. _____ Pisco de guarda is a type of aged pisco produced in Peru.

11. _____ Chile produces a unique type of pisco known as pisco mosto verde.

12. _____ All Chilean pisco must rest for a minimum of sixty days before bottling.

13. _____ The agency CONAPISCO is the governing body for Chilean pisco.

14. _____ Peruvian pisco must be bottled at the same level of alcohol as when it was produced—no additives are allowed.

15. _____ The Tortontel grape used in the production of Chilean pisco is a descendant of a País X Muscat of Alexandria cross.

16. _____ The main grapes used for the production of Chilean pisco include Chardonnay, Sauvignon Blanc, and Sauvignon Vert.

EXERCISE 9: GRAPE BRANDY AROUND THE WORLD: FILL IN THE BLANK/SHORT ANSWER

Fill in the blanks or provide a short answer for the following statements or questions.

1. Fine de la Marne is a good-quality French brandy produced using grapes from the
_____ wine region.

2. What percentage of US brandy is produced in the state of California?
_____

3. What are the two most common grape varieties used in California brandy?
_____

4. The grapes used for California brandy are grown almost exclusively in the
_____ Valley.

5. What two regions are the biggest producers of South African brandy?
_____

6. South African pot still brandy must be _____% pot still brandy and must be aged for a minimum of
_____ years in oak barrels.

7. South African blended brandy must contain a minimum of _____% pot still brandy.

8. South African vintage brandy is produced from a blend of column still brandy and pot still brandy, both of
which must have been aged for a minimum of _____ years.

9. German brandies labeled with the term _____ must be aged for a minimum
of six months in wood; those labeled with the term _____ must be aged for a minimum of
twelve months in wood.

10. Metaxa, produced in _____, is a brandy product infused with _____,
and is blended with Muscat wine.

11. El Presidente Brandy is produced in _____.

12. Aguardente da Vinho Lourinhã DOC brandy is produced in the _____ region of
_____.

13. Australian brandy with the phrase *Very Old* on the label must be aged for a minimum of _____
years in wood.

14. Singani is a grape brandy produced in _____.

EXERCISE 10: POMACE BRANDY AND FRUIT BRANDY: MATCHING

Match each the following terms with its appropriate definition. Terms will be used only once.

Grappa   Monovitigno   Bourgogne
Eaux-de-vie de marc   Nonino   Geist
Stravecchia   Orujo   Mirabelle
Resentin   Picolit   Quetsch
Caffè corretto   Invecchiata   Slivovitz

1. _____   Grappa that has been aged for a minimum of eighteen months in wood

2. _____   Region well-known for producing high-quality pomace brandy in France

3. _____   Distillery that pioneered the single-variety style of grappa

4. _____   A French brandy made from yellow plums

5. _____   A pomace brandy produced in Spain

6. _____   A shot of grappa served in a shot of espresso

7. _____   Term that means "grape stalk" in Italian

8. _____   Grape variety used to produce the first single-variety grappa in 1973

9. _____   A plum brandy produced in Alsace

10. _____   A single-grape variety of grappa

11. _____   Grappa that has been aged for a minimum of twelve months in wood

12. _____   A shot of espresso followed by a shot of grappa (swirled in the same cup)

13. _____   Term used for French brandies distilled from pomace

14. _____   A brandy made from plums that is produced in Croatia, Slovakia, and other countries in central and eastern Europe

15. _____   EU term for a product made by macerating fruit in neutral spirits

EXERCISE 11: CALVADOS AND APPLE BRANDY: MATCHING

Match each of the following terms with its appropriate definition. Terms may be used more than once.

Calvados AOC   Mistelle   Foudres
Calvados Pays d'Auge AOC   Pommeau   Freeze distillation
Calvados Domfrontais AOC   Jack Rose   Blended applejack
Calvados Fermier   Apple brandy

1. _____   Type of calvados that makes up over 70% of the total production of calvados

2. _____   A spirit produced in Normandy from unfermented apple juice and calvados

3. _____   Traditional method used to produce American applejack

4. _____   Type of calvados that requires a minimum of three years of oak aging

5. _____   Term that, according to TTB standards, is synonymous with "applejack"

6. _____   Type of calvados that must be produced using column still distillation

7. _____   Large oak barrels traditionally used to age calvados

8. _____   General French term for fruit juice whose fermentation has been halted by the addition of spirits

9. _____   Method of distillation also known as congelation

10. _____ A classic cocktail made with applejack, lemon juice, and grenadine

11. _____ Type of calvados that must be distilled in an alembic pot still

12. _____ A type of farmer-produced calvados made using traditional agricultural methods

13. _____ A mixture of 20% applejack and 80% neutral spirits

14. _____ Type of calvados that requires the use of a minimum of 30% pear cider

1. What type of fruit is used to produce "Williams" spirit?
   a. Grapes
   b. Apricots
   c. Pears
   d. Plums

2. Which of the following regions is considered to produce the finest cognac?
   a. Petite Champagne
   b. Grande Champagne
   c. Bon Bois
   d. Fin Bois

3. What is the main grape variety used in the production of cognac?
   a. Sémillon
   b. Folle Blanche
   c. Folignan
   d. Ugni Blanc

4. What is the minimum amount of aging time required for three-star (VS) cognac?
   a. Six months
   b. One year
   c. Two years
   d. Three years

5. What is the minimum amount of aging time required for hors d'age cognac?
   a. Six years
   b. Eight years
   c. Ten years
   d. Twenty years

6. Which of the following regions is considered to produce the finest armagnac?
   a. Ténarèze
   b. Borderies
   c. Bas-Armagnac
   d. Haut-Armagnac

7. Which of the following is a hybrid grape variety used in the production of armagnac?
   a. Folle Blanche
   b. Noah
   c. Colombard
   d. Baco Blanc

8. Which of the following is the preferred type of wood for the aging of armagnac?
   a. Monlezun oak
   b. American oak
   c. Chestnut
   d. Cherry

9. What is the minimum required aging time for three-star (VS) armagnac?
   a. One year
   b. Two years
   c. Three years
   d. Four years

10. Which of the following is the main grape variety used in brandy de Jerez?
    a. Ugni Blanc
    b. Palomino
    c. Airén
    d. Trebbiano Toscano

11. Which of the following spirits—as used in the production of brandy de Jerez—has the lowest potential alcohol by volume?
    a. Destilado
    b. Alquitaras
    c. Holandas
    d. Aguardiente

12. Which of the following ingredients are included in the recipe for a Peruvian Pisco Sour?
    a. Lime juice, simple syrup, and egg white
    b. Lemon juice, cream, and simple syrup
    c. Granulated sugar, orange juice, and egg white
    d. Cream, powdered sugar, and key lime juice

13. Which of the following products is not permitted to be aged in wood?
    a. Grappa
    b. Chilean Pisco
    c. Brandy de Jerez
    d. Peruvian Pisco

14. Which of the following areas produces the majority of the grapes for use in California brandy?
    a. San Joaquin Valley
    b. Sonoma Valley
    c. Santa Ynez Valley
    d. Lompoc Valley

15. Which of the following products must be aged for a minimum of three years in oak?
    a. VSOP armagnac
    b. Solera Reserva brandy
    c. Pisco de guarda
    d. South African pot still brandy

16. What is the minimum required aging for Asbach Uralt?
    a. Six months in wood
    b. One year in wood
    c. Two years total, with one year in wood
    d. Four years total, with two years in wood

17. Where is Metaxa produced?
    a. Greece
    b. Portugal
    c. Australia
    d. Austria

18. Which of the following types of apples generally makes up the largest proportion of apples for use in calvados?
    a. Acidic/sour
    b. Bittersweet
    c. Yellow rose
    d. Galloway Pippin

19. Which of the following types of calvados must be produced using a minimum of 30% pear cider?
    a. Pommeau de Normandie
    b. Calvados Fermier
    c. Calvados Domfrontais
    d. Calvados Pays d'Auge

20. What is a foudre?
    a. A large oak barrel used to age calvados
    b. A stainless steel container use to produce the base ferment for cognac
    c. The medium-sized barrels used to age brandy de Jerez
    d. Glass bottles used to store and age very old cognac

RUM AND OTHER SUGARCANE-BASED SPIRITS

LEARNING OBJECTIVES

After studying this chapter, the candidate should be able to do the following:
- Define rum in terms of base materials, distillation processes, maturation, and other post-distillation procedures.
- Compare and contrast "agricultural" rum and "industrial" rum.
- Describe the types of rum produced in the various rum-producing regions of the world.
- Identify and discuss the different styles of rum in light of flavor profile and aging regimen.
- Discuss the various other types of sugarcane-based spirits available, including Ronmiel de Canarias, batavia arrack, Seco Herrerano, and tuzemák.
- Discuss the sensory evaluation of rum and the typical procedures for the serving of rum and rum-based drinks.

EXERCISE 1: THE DEFINITION OF RUM: TRUE OR FALSE

Mark each of the following statements as true or false.

1. _____ In the United States, overproof rum is often bottled at 151 proof.

2. _____ Rum made in the United States must be distilled at less than 190 proof.

3. _____ Agricultural rum, or rhum agricole, is produced using raw sugarcane juice.

4. _____ In the United States, flavored rum must be bottled at a minimum of 35% abv.

5. _____ Rum produced in the United States must be bottled at a minimum of 40% abv.

6. _____ Most styles of rum sold in the United States are bottled at 40–50% abv.

7. _____ EU rum must be distilled at less than 190 proof.

8. _____ In most cases, rum with a proof higher than 155 is not permitted to enter the United States.

9. _____ Industrial rum is produced from molasses.

10. _____ Rum produced in the European Union must be bottled at a minimum of 35% abv.

11. _____ EU rum may be produced from sugarcane, sugar beets, or potatoes.

12. _____ Rum produced in the United States must be aged for a minimum of one year.

EXERCISE 2: THE PRODUCTION OF RUM: FILL IN THE BLANK/SHORT ANSWER

Fill in the blanks or provide a short answer for the following statements or questions.

1. Sugarcane is a tall perennial grass plant of the _____ family.

2. In general, when harvested sugarcane leaves the field, its weight is between _____ and _____ percent sugar.

3. Once milling and crushing are completed, raw sugarcane juice has a sugar concentration of about _____ percent.

4. About 10% of all rum produced is made with _____, as opposed to molasses.

5. During the sugar production process, the juice will be concentrated via _____ until the sugar concentration approaches 60%. At this point it is referred to as _____ _____.

6. _____ molasses contains the highest percentage of remaining fermentable sugar; the type of molasses that is lowest in quality and sugar content is referred to as _____.

7. When cultured yeasts are used to ferment the mash, fermentation is usually completed in _____ days.

8. Some styles of rum are produced using _____ fermentation, which relies on wild, naturally occurring yeast.

9. Slower fermentations promote the creation of more _____, which gives the resulting rum more _____ character and fuller flavor.

10. The use of _____ distillation will result in a rum with a lighter style and flavor, while the use of _____ stills are ideal for the production of richer, aged styles of rum.

11. Rum that is aged in wooden barrels, particularly those rums aged in the tropical climate of many rum-producing regions, may lose up to _____ percent of its volume per year.

12. In some styles of rum distillation, a series of copper vessels known as _____ are placed between the pot still and the condenser.

EXERCISE 3: RUM AND OTHER SUGAR-BASED SPIRITS FROM AROUND THE WORLD: MATCHING

Match each of the following terms with its appropriate definition. Terms may be used more than once.

Privateer	Seco Herrerano	Mount Gay	Penny Blue
Tuzemák	Barbancourt	Cachaça	Carúpano
Batavia arrack	Ronmiel de Canarias	Bacardi	El Dorado
Demerara Distillers	Thomas Tew	Flor de Caña	

1. _____   Brand of rum produced in Barbados

2. _____   A rum-based liqueur flavored with honey

3. _____   A brand of Venezuelan rum

4. _____   An Indonesian spirit produced with sugarcane and red rice

5. _____   Company that owns the last fully working wooden Coffey still in existence

6. _____   The world's oldest documented rum brand

7. _____   A sugarcane-based spirit produced in Panama

8. _____   Brand of rum produced in Haiti

9. _____   A New England–style rum produced in Massachusetts

10. _____   Brand of rum produced in Cataño, Puerto Rico

11. _____   A New England–style rum produced in Rhode Island

12. _____   Brand of rum produced in Guyana

13. _____   A traditional Czech spirit produced from sugar beets or potatoes

14. _____   The main ingredient in the popular Caipirinha cocktail

15. _____   Brand of rum produced in Mauritius

16. _____   Brand of rum produced in Nicaragua

EXERCISE 4: RUM FROM JAMAICA AND MARTINIQUE: FILL IN THE BLANK/SHORT ANSWER

Fill in the blanks or provide a short answer for the following statements or questions.

1. Jamaican rum is unique in that the yeast-rich foam leftover from distillation, known as _____, is sometimes used in the rum-production process.

2. Jamaican rum is sometimes produced using _____, the sugar- and mineral-rich froth residue created during the boiling and concentration of sugarcane juice.

3. Traditional Jamaican rum is distilled in _____ and is known for its high concentration of the aromatic compounds known as _____.

4. Jamaican rums in the category of _____ have the lowest level of esters and are known for having light, floral aromas.

5. Jamaican rums with a medium level of esters are known as _____ and tend to have aromas of _____ fruit.

6. Jamaican rums with medium-high ester content are known as _____ and are more aromatic, flavorful, and structured.

7. The highest-ester rums produced in Jamaica are known as _____ _____ and often show pungent _____ aromas when full strength.

8. In what year was the Geographical Indication for Jamaica Rum established? _____.

9. Rhum Martinique AOC is distilled to about _____ % abv in order to retain more of the original flavor of the sugarcane.

10. Rhum Martinique Blanc must be aged for at least _____ weeks.

11. Rhum Martinique Élevé Sous Bois must be aged for a minimum of _____ months in oak barrels.

12. Rhum Martinique Ambré may also be referred to as _____ and requires a minimum of _____ oak aging.

13. Rhum Martinique Vieux must be aged for a minimum of _____ in oak barrels.

14. Rhum Martinique may use the labeling term "VSOP" is it has been oak-aged for a minimum of _____; the term "XO" requires a minimum of _____.

1. Which of the following holds the only AOC for rum in existence?
   a. Guadeloupe
   b. Brazil
   c. Martinique
   d. Jamaica

2. Which of the following types of Jamaican rum would be expected to have the highest level of esters?
   a. Common cleans
   b. Plummers
   c. Blancas
   d. Wedderburns

3. What is the oldest documented rum brand in the world?
   a. Mount Gay
   b. Thomas Tew
   c. La Favorite
   d. Demerara

4. Which of the following types of rum is most likely to be produced using raw sugarcane juice?
   a. Industrial rum
   b. Cachaça
   c. Prichard's
   d. Privateer

5. Of the following places, where is "British style" rum most likely to be produced?
   a. Colombia
   b. St. Croix
   c. Martinique
   d. Jamaica

6. Of the following places, where is "French style" rum most likely to be produced?
   a. Guadeloupe
   b. Trinidad
   c. New England
   d. Cuba

7. Of the following places, where is "Cuban style" rum most likely to be produced?
   a. Guyana
   b. Puerto Rico
   c. Barbados
   d. Martinique

8. Which of the following statements is true about rum that has the term *añejo* on the label?
   a. It must be aged for at least one year before bottling.
   b. It must be aged for a total of two years before bottling, with at least one year in an oak barrel.
   c. It must be aged for a total of five years before bottling.
   d. The term *añejo* is not universally regulated when applied to rum, so there is no standard definition.

9. What country produces batavia arrack?
   a. Spain
   b. Panama
   c. Indonesia
   d. Brazil

10. What is the minimum abv for flavored rum produced in the United States?
    a. 30%
    b. 35%
    c. 37.5%
    d. 40%

11. What is the typical brix (sugar) weight of ripe sugarcane as it is harvested for use in the production of rum?
    a. 4–5%
    b. 10–13%
    c. 18–22%
    d. 29–32%

12. Which of the following styles of rum is most likely to be produced using dunder?
    a. Rhum Martinique
    b. Jamaican rum
    c. Puerto Rican rum
    d. Haitian rum

TEQUILA AND OTHER AGAVE-BASED BEVERAGES

CHAPTER EIGHT

LEARNING OBJECTIVES

After studying this chapter, the candidate should be able to do the following:

- Define tequila in terms of base materials, distillation processes, aging, and other post-distillation procedures.
- Compare and contrast tequila and 100% agave tequila.
- Describe the plant known as the *Agave tequilana Weber*.

- Identify and discuss the various styles of tequila in terms of flavor profile, color, and aging regimen.
- Discuss the various other types of agave-based spirits available, including mezcal, raicilla, and sotol.
- Discuss the sensory evaluation of tequila and the typical procedures for the serving of tequila and tequila-based drinks.

EXERCISE 1: THE AGAVE PLANT: TRUE OR FALSE

Mark each of the following statements as true or false.

1. _____ The leaves of the agave plant, known as pencas, grow in the form of a rosette.

2. _____ Blue agave plants can grow to be five to eight feet (1.5 to 2.4 m) in height.

3. _____ Most agave plants used for tequila production are grown from seeds in commercial nurseries.

4. _____ The *Agave tequilana Weber* plant is the only species of agave that is grown in Mexico.

5. _____ The agave plant belongs to the *Asparagaceae* family.

6. _____ The agave plant is classified as a succulent, but it is not a cactus.

7. _____ In order to be used in the production of tequila, the central stem of the agave plant must be harvested before it is allowed to swell with honey water.

8. _____ Approximately 50% of the blue agave cultivated for use in tequila is grown in Nayarit.

9. _____ Agave plants to be used in the production of tequila are injured by having the central flower stalk removed before the plant has a chance to blossom.

10. _____ The swollen portion of the agave heart is sometimes referred to using the term *cabeza*.

11. _____ Blue agave matures very quickly, allowing tequila distillers to harvest a new crop from a single plant every year.

EXERCISE 2: TEQUILA VOCABULARY: MATCHING

Match each of the following terms with its appropriate definition. Terms will be used only once.

Jimador   Hydrolysis   Bagazo
Tequila refino   Aguamiel   Inulin
Tequila primero   Autoclave   Tahona
Rhizome   Horno   El corazón
Mosto   Coa   Hijuelos

1. _____   The fibers left over after the cooked agaves are "juiced"

2. _____   The alcoholic liquid produced via the fermentation of processed agave juice

3. _____   The heart, or desired portion of the distillation run

4. _____   The chemical breakdown of a compound due to a reaction with water

5. _____   The raw form of carbohydrate found in unprocessed agave

6. _____   The distillate created via the first distillation run in the production of tequila

7. _____   A skilled fieldworker who prepares and harvests the agave plants

8. _____   A modern, high-pressure stainless steel oven used to prepare agave

9. _____   A large stone wheel traditionally used to press the cooked agave

10. _____   A traditional steam oven used to cook and prepare agave

11. _____   The distillate created via the second distillation run in the production of tequila

12. _____   A sharp cutting tool used to prepare the agave plants for harvest

13. _____   The raw "juice" of a swollen agave heart, sometimes known as honey water

14. _____   An underground plant stem

15. _____   Shoots that form along the underground stems of the agave plant

Using the diagram and the place-names listed below, identify the regions and cities within the tequila-producing regions of Mexico.

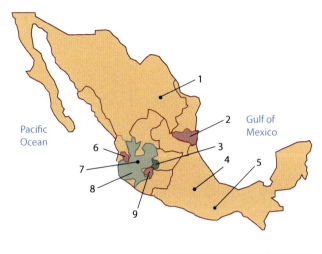

The Tequila-Producing Regions and Mexico: Map Exercise

Copyright: The Society of Wine Educators 2015

Figure 8.1: Tequila Regions and Mexico Map Exercise

1. _____

2. _____

3. _____

4. _____

5. _____

6. _____

7. _____

8. _____

9. _____

Jalisco
Michoacán
Oaxaca
Monterey
Guanajuato
Guadalajara
Mexico City
Tamaulipas
Nayarit

For each of the following statements, determine whether it is true concerning the products of the Amatitán / Lowlands Region or those of Los Altos / the Highlands Region. Place a check mark in the appropriate column.

Statement	The Amatitán / Lowlands Region	Los Altos / the Highlands Region
1. Overall, the warmer of the two regions		
2. Average altitude is 2,000 meters (6,500 feet) above sea level		
3. Produces tequilas that are more vegetal in flavor		
4. Produces tequila with spicy black pepper flavors		
5. Located in the east-central section of Jalisco		
6. Produces tequilas that are highly floral in nature		
7. Produces agave piñas that average 35 to 75 kilos (75 to 165 pounds) in weight		
8. Produces tequilas that are crisper and more earthy		
9. Produces agave piñas that average 50 to 90 kilos (110 to 200 pounds) in weight		
10. Average altitude is 1,300 meters (4,200 feet) above sea level		
11. Produces tequilas that are softer and fruitier		
12. Located in northeastern Jalisco		

EXERCISE 5: BOTTLING AND LABELING TEQUILA: FILL IN THE BLANK/SHORT ANSWER

Fill in the blanks or provide a short answer for the following statements or questions.

1. What are three other terms that may be used on the label of an unaged, or "blanco," tequila?

   _____

2. Mixto (as non-100% agave tequila is often called) must be produced using a minimum of _____% blue agave aguamiel. The remainder of the sugar typically consists of _____.

3. What is the only style of tequila that is not permitted to be mellowed with sugar or other additives?

   _____.

4. What three terms may be used to indicate a product made via the blending of young (blanco) tequila with aged tequila? _____.

5. Mixto tequila made with caramel coloring (or other conditioners) and marketed in the United States as "tequila gold" may also be known as _____.

6. _____ tequila must be aged for a minimum of two months in oak vats or barrels.

7. _____ tequila must be aged in oak barrels for a minimum of one year.

8. _____ tequila must be aged in oak barrels for a minimum of three years.

9. Extra-aged or ultra-aged tequila must be aged in oak barrels no larger than

   _____.

10. Flavored tequila has been on the market since the year _____.

11. All _____ tequila must be distilled and bottled in Mexico, but _____ tequila may be exported in bulk and bottled outside of Mexico.

12. _____ is the top-selling brand of tequila (based on global sales).

EXERCISE 6: OTHER AGAVE-BASED BEVERAGES: MATCHING

Match each of the following terms with its appropriate definition. Terms may be used more than once.

Agave angustifolia   Joven   Pulque
Agave salmiano   Mezcal Ancestral   Raicilla
Añejo   Mezcal Artesanal   Reposado
Bacanora   Oaxaca   Sotol

1. _____   A traditional product of Jalisco allowed to be produced from many varieties of agave (but not allowed to be produced using Blue agave)

2. _____   A distilled spirit produced in the states of Chihuahua, Durango, and Coahuila

3. _____   Variety of agave that is used in the production of close to 90% of all mezcal products

4. _____   Type of mezcal that must be oak-aged for at least one year

5. _____   Type of mezcal that requires the agave to be cooked in pit or cement ovens with no stainless steel allowed, but does not require the use of bagazo

6. _____   A fermented beverage produced from agave

7. _____   Agave spirit named for the town in Sonora where it was first produced

8. _____   The traditional center and leading area of mezcal production

9. _____   Type of mezcal that requires a minimum of two months of oak aging

10. _____   Type of mezcal that requires distillation to be accomplished over a direct fire as well as the use of bagazo

11. _____   Type of mezcal with no aging requirement

12. _____   A distilled spirit produced from the desert spoon plant

13. _____   Variety of agave that is allowed, but not widely used in the production of mezcal

14. _____   Translates as "little root"

15. _____   A milky-looking product that is best while fresh and usually consumed locally

1. What is the minimum required aging for añejo tequila?
   a. Six months in oak barrels
   b. One year in oak barrels
   c. Two years in stainless steel
   d. Two years in oak barrels

2. What type of tequila must be aged for a minimum of two months in oak vats or barrels?
   a. Blanco
   b. Plata
   c. Reposado
   d. Seco

3. Which of the following Mexican states contains an approved tequila-production region?
   a. Guanajuato
   b. Puebla
   c. Sonora
   d. Campeche

4. Which of the following batches of ingredients could be legally used for the production of non-100% agave tequila?
   a. A batch containing 37% blue agave, plus nectar from maguey
   b. A batch containing 75% blue agave, plus nectar from maguey
   c. A batch containing 49% blue agave, plus molasses and corn syrup
   d. A batch containing 51% blue agave, plus molasses, cane syrup, and corn syrup

5. What is a tahona?
   a. A term used for the rosette-shaped center of the agave plant
   b. The raw carbohydrate found in agave
   c. A modern oven used for heating and cooling agave
   d. A large stone wheel traditionally used to crush the cooked agave fibers

6. Which of the following is true concerning the distillation of tequila?
   a. The law requires that all tequila be triple-distilled
   b. The law requires that all blanco tequila be column-distilled
   c. The law does not specify the type of distillation that must be used in the production of tequila
   d. The law does not specify the type of still used in the production of tequila, but the tequila is required to be distilled at or above 190°

7. What is the typical alcohol content of tequila primero?
   a. 8% abv
   b. 25% abv
   c. 50% abv
   d. 72% abv

8. Which of the following is the best description of a mixto tequila marketed in the United States as "gold tequila"?
   a. 100% agave tequila with a small amount of sugar added
   b. Non-100% agave tequila with caramel coloring
   c. Mixto tequila that has been aged for three years or more
   d. Unaged 100% agave tequila mixed with an aged 100% agave tequila

9. Which of the following is true concerning mixto tequila?
   a. It may be conditioned with sugar, but it may not be flavored.
   b. It may not be labeled with the term *reposado*.
   c. It may be exported from Mexico in bulk and then bottled in the United States.
   d. It must be aged for a minimum of one year in oak barrels.

10. Which of the following states is the leading producer of tequila?
    a. Jalisco
    b. Tamaulipas
    c. Yucatán
    d. Nayarit

11. Where is San Luis de la Paz located, and what beverage is produced there?
    a. Guerrero, tequila
    b. Oaxaca, raicilla
    c. Michoacán, mezcal
    d. Guanajuato, mezcal

12. Which of the following distillates is produced from the desert spoon plant?
    a. Mezcal de olla
    b. Sotol
    c. Bacanora
    d. Raicilla

LIQUEURS

CHAPTER NINE

LEARNING OBJECTIVES

After studying this chapter, the candidate should be able to do the following:
- Define the distilled spirit category known as liqueurs in terms of base materials, sweeteners, and flavorings.
- Identify the elements of liqueur flavor and describe the various flavoring procedures used in the production of liqueurs.
- Identify and describe the leading members of the following liqueur categories: fruit liqueurs; herbal liqueurs; bean, nut, and seed liqueurs; cream liqueurs; and whiskey liqueurs.

EXERCISE 1: THE DEFINITION OF LIQUEURS: TRUE OR FALSE

Mark each of the following statements as true or false.

1. _____ In general, the minimum required sugar content for liqueurs is much higher in the United States than it is in the European Union.

2. _____ In the European Union, cherry liqueurs must have a minimum sugar content of 7%.

3. _____ Crème de cassis is flavored with black currant.

4. _____ In the United States, bourbon liqueur must be bottled at a minimum of 40% abv.

5. _____ In the United States, rock and rye liqueur must be at least 51% rye whiskey and be flavored with rock candy or sugar syrup.

6. _____ In the United States, the terms *liqueur* and *cordial* are used interchangeably.

7. _____ In the United States, brandy liqueur must be bottled at a minimum of 35% abv.

8. _____ In the United States, brandy liqueur may be produced using a blend of brandy and neutral spirits as its base.

9. _____ In the European Union, the term *cordial* refers to a nonalcoholic flavoring.

10. _____ EU liqueurs are not allowed to contain any amount of dairy products, including cream.

11. _____ In the European Union, "crème" liqueurs (such as crème de cocoa) must be at least 25% sugar.

12. _____ In the European Union, all liqueurs are required to be bottled at a minimum of 30% abv.

EXERCISE 2: THE PRODUCTION OF LIQUEURS: FILL IN THE BLANK/SHORT ANSWER

Fill in the blanks or provide a short answer for the following statements or questions.

1. The first step in the production of a liqueur is to select the _____
   and the _____.

2. In general, the extraction of fruit flavors in the production of liqueurs is done using one of the
   _____ methods.

3. The gentlest method of flavor extraction is _____. This process is
   accomplished via steeping the flavoring ingredients, such as fruit, in a liquid in order to extract the flavor.

4. In the _____ method of flavor extraction, often used with
   hardier fruits and berries, the flavor source is cut, crushed, or pressed and then steeped in an
   _____ solution.

5. Another method of cold extraction is _____, where a neutral spirit is pumped
   continuously over and passed through the flavoring material.

6. In the _____ method of flavor extraction, essences or concentrates
   are simply blended into a base spirit.

7. The _____ method of flavor extraction, sometimes called distillation, is typically used for
   products flavored with seeds and flowers.

8. In the case of very delicate flowers and herbs, sometimes a process known as
   _____ is used, which permits water to boil at lower temperatures.

9. Once the flavor has integrated, the liqueur is reduced in strength and _____.

10. Some liqueurs are colored with either naturally derived coloring or _____.

11. Most liqueurs are _____, but some are allowed to rest for a period of time in order to allow
    the flavors to mellow.

12. While the various types of liqueurs have different requirements, the usual range for the amount of alcohol
    in a liqueur is from _____ to _____ proof.

EXERCISE 3: FRUIT LIQUEURS: MATCHING

Match each of the following terms with its appropriate definition. Terms may be used more than once.

Chambord   Midori Melon   Cassis
Limoncello   Heering Cherry Liqueur   Malibu
Cointreau   Grand Marnier Cordon Rouge   Triple Sec
Luxardo Maraschino   Grand Marnier Cordon Jaune   Mandarine Napoléon

1. _____   A French orange liqueur that uses cognac as the base spirit

2. _____   A liqueur that was originally produced in the city of Zadar on Croatia's Dalmatian Coast

3. _____   A rum and coconut liqueur produced in Barbados

4. _____   A liqueur produced in the Commune de Cour-Cheverny in the Loire Valley

5. _____   A traditional, often homemade liqueur produced throughout southern Italy

6. _____   An ingredient in the Hemingway Daiquiri and the Mary Pickford cocktail

7. _____   A liqueur named after the Japanese word for "green"

8. _____   A Danish liqueur used in the recipe for the Blood and Sand cocktail

9. _____   A proprietary French liqueur originally produced as a less-sweet alternative to Dutch orange liqueurs

10. _____   A black raspberry flavored liqueur

11. _____   A French orange flavored liqueur intended to be used in recipes including crêpes suzette

12. _____   A tangerine-flavored liqueur originally produced in Belgium

13. _____   A generic term used for orange liqueur

14. _____   Used—along with champagne—in the Kir Royale cocktail

EXERCISE 4: LIQUEURS: MATCHING

Match each of the following terms with its appropriate definition. Terms may be used more than once.

Frangelico   Nocino   Crème Yvette
Southern Comfort   Liquore Strega   Amarula
Drambuie   Domaine de Canton   St. Germain
Goldschläger   Galliano   Kümmel
Disaronno Originale   Tuaca   Bärenfang

1. _____   A liqueur flavored with violet petals and berries

2. _____   An Italian liqueur with a vibrant yellow color due to the addition of saffron

3. _____   A liqueur flavored with elderflowers

4. _____   An Italian liqueur flavored with apricot kernel oil

5. _____   A brandy-based liqueur flavored with vanilla and citrus

6. _____   A German honey-and-vodka liqueur

7. _____   A liqueur based on Swiss cinnamon schnapps

8. _____   A walnut liqueur originally from Italy's Emilia-Romagna region

9. _____   A cream liqueur from South Africa

10. _____   A cognac-based French liqueur flavored with ginger

11. _____   An American liqueur invented in New Orleans

12. _____   A Tuscan liqueur named after an Italian war hero

13. _____   A liqueur made with a Scotch whisky base

14. _____   An Italian liqueur originally from the city of Benevento

15. _____   A liqueur flavored with caraway and cumin

16. _____   A hazelnut-flavored liqueur

1. Which of the following is a cold method of flavor extraction?
   a. Infusion
   b. Maceration
   c. Percolation
   d. All of the above

2. Which of the following is considered the gentlest form of flavor extraction?
   a. Infusion
   b. Maceration
   c. Percolation
   d. Distillation

3. Which of the following is considered a generic liqueur?
   a. Crème Yvette
   b. St. Germain
   c. Malibu rum liqueur
   d. Crème de violette

4. What is the minimum required sugar content for liqueurs produced in the United States?
   a. 1.0%
   b. 2.5%
   c. 10%
   d. 25%

5. In the European Union, what is the minimum sugar content for crème liqueurs?
   a. 7%
   b. 10%
   c. 15%
   d. 25%

6. Which liqueur is flavored with egg yolk?
   a. Sambuca
   b. Advocaat
   c. Nocino
   d. Crème de noisette

7. Which of the following is a Danish producer of spirits and liqueurs?
   a. Peter Heering
   b. Marnier-Lapostolle
   c. Luxardo
   d. Charles Jacquin

8. Which of the following liqueurs is flavored with black currant?
   a. Maraschino
   b. Crème de cassis
   c. Nocino
   d. St. Germain

9. Which of the following is a bourbon liqueur?
   a. Drambuie
   b. Jeremiah Weed
   c. Amarula
   d. Irish Mist

10. Which of the following is a cream liqueur?
    a. Tuaca
    b. Tia Maria
    c. Amarula
    d. Crème de noisette

11. Which of the following liqueurs is colored and flavored with saffron?
    a. Liquore Strega
    b. Grand Marnier Cordon Jaune
    c. Amarula
    d. Goldschläger

12. Which of the following liqueurs is flavored with Alpine elderflowers?
    a. Galliano
    b. Crème Yvette
    c. Domaine de Canton
    d. St. Germain

VERMOUTH, AMARI, AND BITTERS

CHAPTER TEN

LEARNING OBJECTIVES

After studying this chapter, the candidate should be able to do the following:

- Discuss the taste component of bitter and its importance to both the alcoholic beverage industry and mixology.
- Define and discuss the various styles of aromatized wines, including vermouth, vini amari, quinquina, and americano.
- Identify and describe the various types and styles of bittered spirits.
- Describe the leading brands of cocktail bitters and explain their use in cocktails, mixed drinks, and other beverages.

EXERCISE 1: THE DEFINITION OF AROMATIZED WINES: TRUE OR FALSE

Mark each of the following statements as true or false.

1. _____ Aromatized wines are wine-based beverages that are flavored with aromatic botanicals, which may or may not contain added sugar.

2. _____ According to EU standards, aromatized wines must be made from a wine base of at least 90% before enhancement.

3. _____ The minimum alcohol content for an EU aromatized wine labeled with the term *semi-sweet* is 14.5%.

4. _____ EU vermouth is defined as an aromatized wine flavored with artemisia as well as other natural flavorings.

5. _____ A quinquina is an aromatized wine flavored with wormwood and/or gentian.

6. _____ In the European Union, an "extra-dry" aromatized wine must have a sugar content of less than 30 g/L.

7. _____ According to the European Union, sangria may be produced in only Spain, Portugal, or France; otherwise, it must be labeled with the place of origin, as in "German sangria."

8. _____ Bitterness can be discerned at a lower threshold than sweetness, saltiness, and acidity.

9. _____ Cremovo is an egg-based aromatized wine produced exclusively in Madeira.

10. _____ The minimum alcohol content for an EU aromatized wine labeled with the term *dry* is 20%.

11. _____ In the European Union, an aromatized wine labeled with the term *sweet* must have a minimum sugar content of 130 g/L.

12. _____ Many aromatized wines may also be classified as fortified wines.

Match each of the following terms with its appropriate definition. Terms may be used more than once.

Primitivo Quiles   Boissiere   Carpano Antica Formula
Yzaguirre   Vermouth di Torino   Vermouth de Chambéry
Atsby Vermouth   Ransom Vermouth   Lustau
Noilly Prat   Dolin   Casa Mariol
Stock Spirits Group   Carpano Punt e Mes

1. _____ A Spanish vermouth that uses a red wine made using the Mourvèdre grape variety as its base

2. _____ A vermouth produced with natural vanilla flavoring

3. _____ An Italian vermouth with PGI status

4. _____ A Spanish vermouth produced in Tarragona, often cited for its "balsamic" character

5. _____ A company known for producing Torino-style vermouth in the city of Trieste

6. _____ A company that produces several styles of Vermouth de Chambéry as well as Chambéryzette

7. _____ A Spanish vermouth produced in the Alicante region

8. _____ A type of vermouth known as "vermouth with bitters"

9. _____ A New World–style vermouth produced in New York City

10. _____ A Spanish vermouth produced in a style known as "vermut negre"

11. _____ A company that produces a dry white vermouth in the style of Vermouth de Chambéry (but actually produced in the city of Turin)

12. _____ A New World–style vermouth produced in Oregon

13. _____ A producer of Marseilles-style vermouth

14. _____ A producer of Sherry and Sherry-based vermouth

15. _____ A style of vermouth produced in the French Alps

EXERCISE 3: VINI AMARI, QUINQUINA, AND AMERICANO: FILL IN THE BLANK/SHORT ANSWER

Fill in the blanks or provide a short answer for the following statements or questions.

1. Barolo Chinato, produced in the _____ region of Italy, is one example of a traditional beverage known as _____, which means (basically) "bitter and herbal."

2. Quinquina wines are flavored and fortified, and use _____ bark as the primary botanical.

3. _____ is a reddish-brown quinquina produced using gentian root, cinchona, and a variety of herbs from the Chartreuse Mountains.

4. A quinquina known as _____ is produced in the Roussillon region of France, using a mistelle made primarily of _____ and _____ grapes.

5. A French doctor created a quinquina known as _____, named in honor of an angel that he claimed healed his sight.

6. _____ is a mild quinquina produced in Podensac, Bordeaux. The original product, based on white Bordeaux wine, was known as _____.

7. A limited-edition quinquina known as _____ is based on Sauternes.

8. One of the lighter products in the quinquina category, _____ was originally produced in France and is now also made at the Heaven Hills Distillery in Kentucky.

9. Americano is a category of aromatized wines flavored with both _____ and _____.

10. The category of americano wines should not be confused with the Americano cocktail, which is a concoction of sweet red vermouth, soda, citrus peel, and _____.

11. The classic white version of _____ is often mentioned as a substitute for the original (and no longer produced) Kina Lillet.

12. The _____ Winery produces a version of americano known as _____, which is made using wine made from the Cortese grape variety.

EXERCISE 4: SPIRIT AMARI: MATCHING

Match each of the following terms with its appropriate definition. Terms may be used more than once.

Suze   Picon   Jägermeister
Gammel Dansk   Chartreuse   Cynar
Bénédictine   Fernet Branca   Averna
Zwack Unicum   Aperol   Negroni
Becherovka   Campari

1. _____   A French amer that is part of the recipe known as the Basque national drink

2. _____   The top-selling bittered spirit in the world

3. _____   A bold, bittered liqueur produced in Budapest

4. _____   An Italian amari with an intense bitter orange flavor; one of the first amari to become popular outside of Europe

5. _____   A French amer that is part of the recipe for the Vieux Carré cocktail

6. _____   A cocktail produced with Campari, sweet vermouth, and gin

7. _____   A French amer that is produced in several styles, including a special bottling known as VEP

8. _____   A French amer that gained a great reputation when it appeared in a painting by Pablo Picasso

9. _____   A very popular Italian amari originally produced in Milan

10. _____   A bittered spirit produced in the Czech Republic

11. _____   A French amer originally produced by the monks of the Carthusian Order

12. _____   A rich, brown-hued Italian amari flavored with licorice, cola, sassafras, chocolate, and Sicilian herbs

13. _____   An Italian amari flavored with bitter oranges; intended to be slightly less bitter and lower in alcohol than most

14. _____   A bittered spirit that is often served with birthday breakfasts in Denmark

15. _____   An Italian amari flavored with artichokes

1. According to EU standards, aromatized wines must be produced from a base consisting of at least _____ wine (before enhancement).
   a. 25%
   b. 35%
   c. 50%
   d. 75%

2. What is the required sugar content for EU aromatized wines that are labeled with the term *semi-sweet*?
   a. Less than 50 g/L
   b. Between 50 g/L and 90 g/L
   c. Between 90 g/L and 130 g/L
   d. Between 130 g/L and 140 g/L

3. The German product known as maiwein (May wine) must be flavored with which of the following botanicals?
   a. Sweet woodruff
   b. Wormwood
   c. Gentian
   d. Elderflower

4. Which of the following is a white-wine-based beverage flavored with honey and spices?
   a. Zurra
   b. Clarea
   c. Sangria
   d. Glühwein

5. Which of the following products is produced by Lustau?
   a. Premium red sherry vermouth
   b. New world vermouth
   c. Barolo Chinato
   d. Red vermouth from Torino

6. What type of product is produced by the Dolin House?
   a. Vermouth di Torino
   b. Spanish vermouth
   c. Vermouth de Chambéry
   d. Trieste Vermouth

7. Which of the following products is a vermouth flavored with vanilla?
   a. Noilly Prat
   b. Carpano Antica Formula
   c. Punt e Mes
   d. Chamberyzette

8. Which of the following is an americano?
   a. St. Raphael
   b. Dubonnet
   c. Contratto
   d. Campari

9. Which of the following is a carciofo?
   a. Averna
   b. Suze
   c. Cynar
   d. Picon

10. Which of the following is, by way of a well-known recipe, made into a "spritz" with Prosecco and soda?
    a. Aperol
    b. Averna
    c. Amaro Nonino
    d. Becherovka

11. Which of the following was introduced to the world at the 1967 World Expo in Montreal, where it was made into a cocktail with tonic?
    a. Becherovka
    b. Gammel Dansk
    c. Averna
    d. Campari

12. Which of the following is a French amer that also comes in a sweeter, yellow version flavored with saffron?
    a. Bénédictine
    b. Picon
    c. Unicum
    d. Chartreuse

MIXOLOGY

LEARNING OBJECTIVES

After studying this chapter, the candidate should be able to do the following:

- Identify the key ingredients, glassware, and equipment needed to properly stock a full-service bar.
- Compare and contrast cocktails and mixed drinks, citing several examples of each.
- Discuss the various mixing methods used in the preparation of drinks, and identify the style of drinks best prepared by each.
- Identify and describe the twelve basic drink families.
- Describe the importance of responsible beverage alcohol service.

EXERCISE 1: MIXOLOGY: TRUE OR FALSE

Mark each of the following statements as true or false.

1. _____ According to one of the earliest definitions, a "cocktail" contained spirits, sugar, water, and bitters.

2. _____ The term *cocktail* specifically refers to a tall mixed drink made by combining one spirit and one mixer over ice.

3. _____ The typical shelf life of house-made simple syrup is one year.

4. _____ Tinctures are useful in that they can add a specific, concentrated flavor to a drink without increasing its volume or diluting the other flavors.

5. _____ The flavor of lemon juice will begin to deteriorate after twelve hours, while orange juice is usually able to last at least twice that long.

6. _____ Infusions, made with neutral spirits and selected flavorings, are similar to tinctures, but infusions are much more concentrated.

7. _____ Jerry Thomas, considered to be the forefather of today's modern mixologists, published *The Bartender's Guide* in the 1860s.

8. _____ The "back bar" area of an establishment should be arranged in such a way as to promote sales and market premium products.

9. _____ The basic recipe for simple syrup is one-to-one—for instance, one cup of sugar dissolved in one cup of water.

10. _____ The Sazerac, one of the original American cocktails, was invented in New Orleans.

11. _____ Small ice cubes melt slower than large ice cubes and release less water into a drink.

EXERCISE 2: MODERN MIXOLOGY AND CRAFT COCKTAILS: FILL IN THE BLANK/SHORT ANSWER

Fill in the following chart with the missing terms.

	A pre-Prohibition cocktail made with rum, spruce beer, and molasses
	A special bar tool used to crush ingredients such as mint leaves or lime wedges in order to squeeze out juices, oils, and flavors
	A beverage made in colonial America using the liquid from a batch of fruit macerated with sugar and vinegar
	To make and mix drinks without using any kind of measuring device or measured pour spout
	Measurement of the weight of a liquid in reference to water
	The peel of a citrus fruit specially cut to be used as a drink garnish
	A drink popular in colonial America often made (as the legend goes) by Martha Washington using cherries, spices, and a bottle of rye whiskey
	Term often used to describe a shot of liquor poured directly into the glass
	A classic cocktail originally prepared with cognac, orange liqueur, bitters, and lemon juice, garnished with a long loop of lemon peel and a sugared rim
	Term used to describe a drink that is shaken or stirred with ice to chill, strained into the glass, and served without ice
	Vintage cocktails made with a base spirit or wine, sugar, and fruit shaken with ice and poured, unstrained, into a glass; original version made with sherry
	Term used for the last (lightest) ingredient to be poured in a layered drink
	A classic cocktail made with gin (or another spirit), lemon juice, and sugar, shaken with an egg white and served tall over ice with carbonated water
	Modern term used for a nonalcoholic drink served alongside a shot or a strong drink

EXERCISE 3: MIXING METHODS: MATCHING

Match each of the following terms with its appropriate definition or statement. Terms may be used more than once.

Build	Stir	Dry shake
Blend	Shake	Roll

1. _____   Used for cocktails made with two or more easily blended ingredients

2. _____   The best choice to use when making a Bloody Mary

3. _____   The best choice to use when following a recipe that contains egg whites

4. _____   The best choice to use in order to make a Martini with an airy texture

5. _____   The best choice for making a rum and Coke

6. _____   The best mixing choice for making an ice cream-based Brandy Alexander

7. _____   The best choice for making cocktails that contain sugar or heavy cream

8. _____   Used when making drinks by placing spirits, ice, and mixers directly into the serving glass

9. _____   Method of mixing drinks sometimes known as the pouring method

10. _____   The best mixing method to use when starting to make a Peruvian Pisco Sour

11. _____   Ideal method to use with ingredients that may create an unattractive foam when shaken

12. _____   The best choice for making a frozen Strawberry Margarita

13. _____   The best choice for making a Tequila Sunrise

14. _____   The best choice to use when starting to make a Silver Fizz

Match the following drinks with their appropriate family. Terms may be used more than once.

Sours	Pousse-cafés	Wines and punches
Shooters	The Martini family	Cream-based drinks
Highballs	Two-liquor drinks on ice	Tropical drinks

1. _____ Margarita

2. _____ Black Russian

3. _____ Rob Roy

4. _____ Lemon Drop

5. _____ Kir

6. _____ Mudslide

7. _____ Mimosa

8. _____ Grasshopper

9. _____ Hemingway Daiquiri

10. _____ Rusty Nail

11. _____ Angel's Kiss

12. _____ Manhattan

13. _____ Jack and Ginger

14. _____ Piña Colada

15. _____ Gimlet

1. Which of the following beverages would most accurately be considered a cocktail as opposed to a mixed drink?
   a. Rum and Coke
   b. Tequila Sunrise
   c. Manhattan
   d. Bloody Mary

2. Which of the following beverages would most accurately be considered a mixed drink as opposed to a cocktail?
   a. Peruvian Pisco Sour
   b. Rob Roy
   c. Lemon Drop
   d. Jack and Ginger

3. Which of the following vintage cocktails is produced using rum, spruce beer, and molasses?
   a. Cobbler
   b. Calibogus
   c. Sangaree
   d. Shrub

4. What should be considered the maximum shelf life for freshly squeezed lemon juice?
   a. Eight hours
   b. Twenty-four hours
   c. Two days
   d. One week

5. Tequila that has been macerated with fresh sage for three weeks is an example of which of the following products?
   a. An infusion
   b. A tincture
   c. Cocktail bitters
   d. Premade cocktails

6. What is the proper bar term to use for a drink that has been shaken or stirred with ice to chill, and then strained and served without ice?
   a. Neat
   b. Tall
   c. Up
   d. Light

7. Which drink-mixing procedure is best to use for a customer wanting a Martini with a light, airy texture?
   a. Stir
   b. Blend
   c. Dry shake
   d. Shake

8. Which drink-mixing procedure is best to use for preparing a Tequila Sunrise?
   a. Stir
   b. Build
   c. Dry shake
   d. Blend

9. The preparation of which of the following drinks would most likely require the use of a Hawthorne strainer?
   a. Martini (shaken)
   b. Scotch Mist
   c. Bloody Mary
   d. Tequila Sunrise

10. Which of the following drinks is a member of the "sours" family?
    a. Margarita
    b. Rob Roy
    c. Manhattan
    d. Rusty Nail

IMPACT OF ALCOHOL ON HEALTH

CHAPTER TWELVE

LEARNING OBJECTIVES

After studying this chapter, the candidate should be able to do the following:

- Recognize the potential negative consequences of excessive alcohol consumption.

- Discuss the potential health benefits of the moderate intake of alcohol.
- Understand how to achieve a healthy balance between the risks and benefits associated with alcohol consumption.

EXERCISE 1: THE IMPACT OF ALCOHOL ON HEALTH: FILL IN THE BLANK/SHORT ANSWER

Fill in the blanks for the following statements or questions.

1. _____, the by-product produced when alcohol is metabolized in the liver, can build up in the bloodstream and cause _____.

2. _____, defined as consuming large amounts of alcohol one or two nights a week, is one of the leading causes of death among young people.

3. The USDA recommends _____ drink per day for women, and _____ drinks per day for men, as a definition of "moderate consumption."

4. The definition of "one serving" of wine (at 12–14% abv) is _____.

5. The definition of "one serving" of beer (at 5% abv) is _____.

6. The definition of "one serving" of spirits (at 40% abv) is _____.

7. Some studies have shown that a decreased risk of coronary heart disease correlates with moderate drinking, most likely due to the _____- and _____-reducing effects of alcohol.

8. It is important to remember that alcohol _____ blood pressure.

9. Excessive amounts of alcohol can lead to _____, a condition where fat accumulates within the cells of the liver.

10. _____ is a nonreversible liver condition that can result from excessive alcohol consumption.

11. _____ is a beneficial phenolic compound found in red wine that has been shown to have anti-aging and disease-fighting properties.

1. Which of the following is considered to be a generally safe level of "moderate drinking," as defined by the USDA?
   a. Up to one drink a day for both men and women
   b. Up to two drinks a day for both men and women
   c. Up to one drink a day for women, and up to two drinks a day for men
   d. Up to one drink a day for men, and up to two drinks a day for women

2. Which of the following is considered to be "one serving" of wine (at 12% to 14% abv), as defined by the USDA?
   a. 4 ounces
   b. 5 ounces
   c. 8 ounces
   d. 10 ounces

3. Which of the following is considered to be "one serving" of beer (at 5% abv), as defined by the USDA?
   a. 12 ounces
   b. 14 ounces
   c. 16 ounces
   d. 20 ounces

4. Which of the following is considered to be "one serving" of spirits (at 40% abv), as defined by the USDA?
   a. ¾ ounce
   b. 1 ounce
   c. 1½ ounces
   d. 2 ounces

5. The practice of "saving up" one's alcohol consumption for one night a week is best described by which of the following terms?
   a. Binge drinking
   b. Moderate consumption
   c. Chronic consumption
   d. Depressive consumption

6. Alcohol-related intoxication occurs as which of the following substances is built up in the bloodstream?
   a. Resveratrol
   b. Acetaldehyde
   c. Methanol
   d. Inulin

7. Which of the following patterns of alcohol consumption has shown to have the greatest health benefits over time?
   a. Consistently consuming the same type of alcohol
   b. Finding the specific brand of spirit that has the least noticeable effects on one's mood
   c. Only consuming alcohol on a sporadic basis
   d. Consuming alcohol only with meals, at the same time each day

8. Studies have shown that consuming just over _____ of ethanol each day is enough to potentially lead to the condition known as fatty liver.
   a. 25 ml
   b. 50 ml
   c. 100 ml
   d. 200 ml

9. Which of the following is the most dramatic effect of alcohol on the human body?
   a. Depressant
   b. Anti-inflammatory
   c. Stimulant
   d. Antioxidant

10. Cirrhosis is a potentially fatal disease that primarily impacts which of the following organs?
    a. Brain
    b. Liver
    c. Thyroid
    d. Heart

CERTIFIED SPECIALIST OF SPIRITS

ADDITIONAL MATERIALS: BLANK MAPS

Whisky-Producing Regions
of Scotland

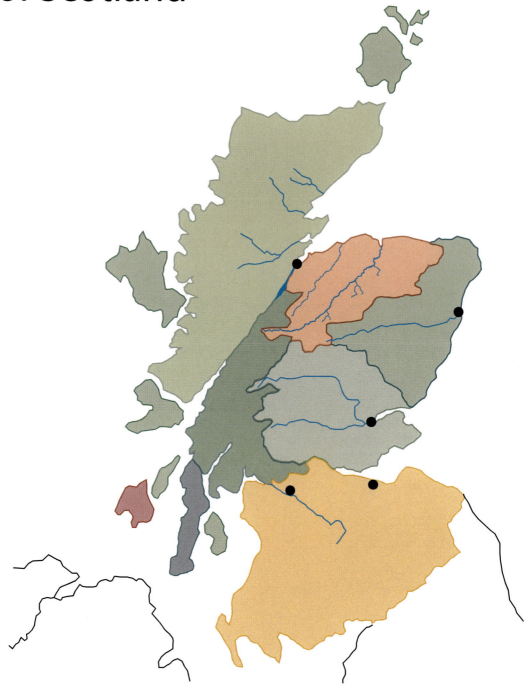

Figure A.1: Blank Map of the Whisky-Producing Regions of Scotland

The Cognac Region

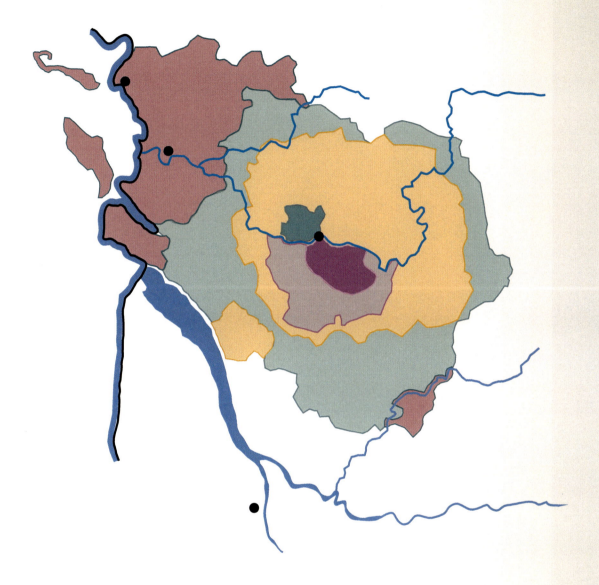

Figure A.2: Blank Map of the Cognac Region

The Armagnac Region

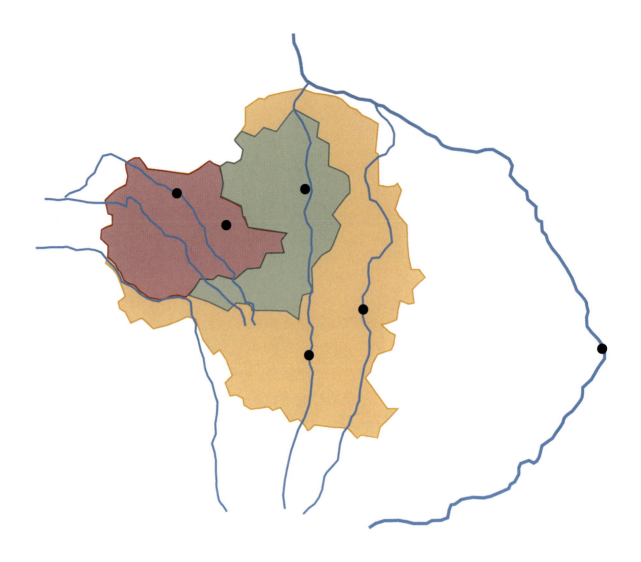

Figure A.3: Blank Map of the Armagnac Region

Tequila-Producing Regions

Figure A.4: Blank Map of the Tequila-Producing Regions of Mexico